I0568602

# Z 2 A

## Eva Dillner

## Books by Eva Dillner

new editions in print, audio and e-book formats

### in English

**Z 2 A** (2011)

**Meandering Mind** (2010)
1st edition **The Pathfinder Process** (2005)

**Secrets of Transformation** (2008)
1st edition **The Naked Truth** (2003)

**God put a Dream in my Heart** (2003)

**Mystical Art 2011 Calendar**
**Healing Art 2010 Calendar**
**Art of Now 2009 Calendar**

### in Swedish

**Våga Leva** (2006)
**Livs Levande Eva** (2006)

# Z 2 A

## by Eva Dillner

DIVINE DESIGN
www.evadillner.com

ISBN: 978-91-978231-3-5 (Perfect Bound Color Interior)
ISBN: 978-91-978231-4-2 (digital audio)
ISBN: 978-91-978231-5-9 (e-book)

Printed in the USA by Lightning Source
Digital audio available via Audible, Elib
E-book available via Kindle, Elib, Ingram and Apple

Published by DIVINE DESIGN
www.evadillner.com
Grönhögen, Sweden

# Table of Contents

# We Know How to Achieve

In the West, we know how to achieve - in spades! We know how to plan and execute. We know how to set goals and objectives. We know how to live life from A to Z.

But how do we get from Z to A? What do we know of navigating that space in between? When life as we know it ends, before we see a new beginning, there is a creative void where all things are possible. That's what this book is about.

I call it Z 2 A.

How can we navigate in that uncertain territory, when the path forward is not clear? When the project is finished, or the rug has been pulled out from under us - it doesn't matter if it's a small ending or a life crisis - the process is the same. We are finished with what we were doing. The objectives have been met, the goals achieved, the challenge overcome, the project completed.

Now what? Confusion may set in, or lethargy, or chaos. Our schooling has not prepared us for this. We've been taught that life is a steady path forward. If you've lived awhile you already know this is a lie. Life is not a constant. It's a never ending variation. It doesn't stay the same.

The space in between is that moment when all things are possible. It's the creative void that artists work with. It's the moment of surrender where healing can take place. It's the instant of inspiration where new ideas are born. It's the crack in the wall where change can seep in. It's the chink in the armor where old patterns can be dismantled.

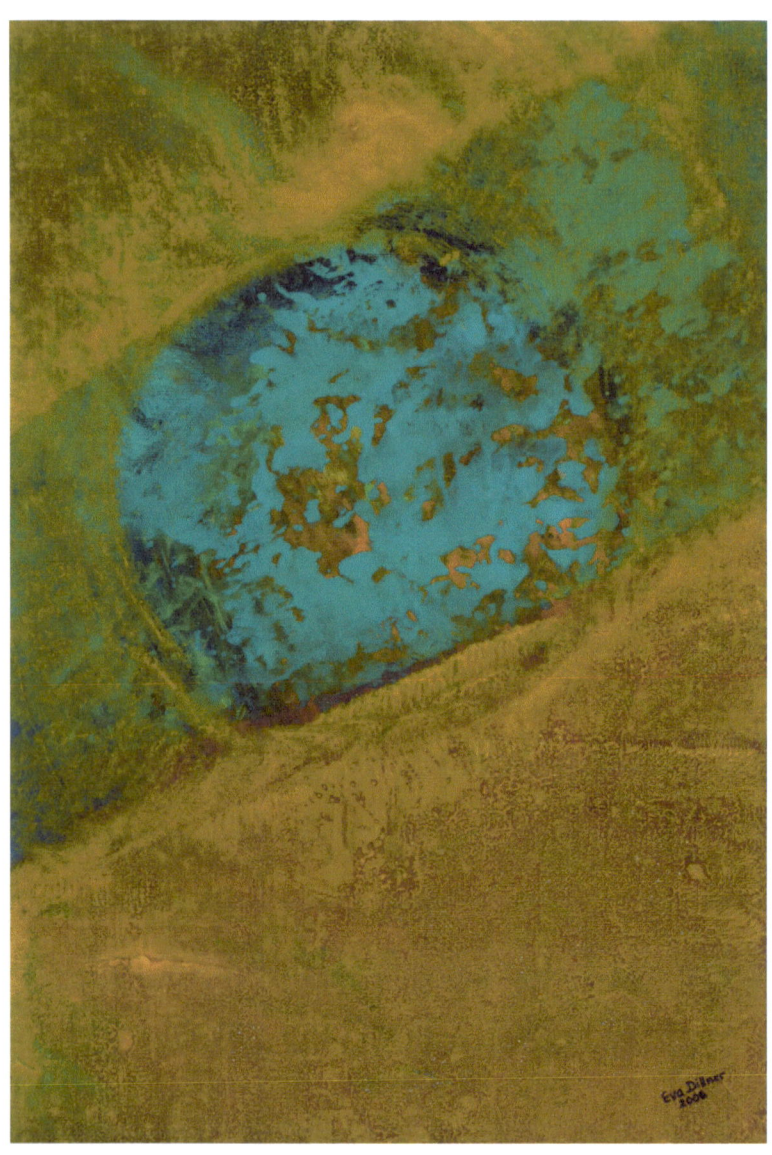

**Z 2 A IS BEYOND TIME AND SPACE**

Understanding and learning to dance in the space in between is useful for everyone. It's a priceless tool that we all can use in relationships, at work, with healing, in creative endeavors as well as government structures. From the art of creating a garden to shaping a new world, the process is the same. It doesn't matter if it's big or small.

Learning to hang out in the space in between Z and A is essential to the future of the planet. So come explore with me. Come play with the possibilities. Come discover moments where all things are possible. Where new solutions appear. Where creativity blooms. Where the life energy flows freely, in stillness and chaos. Come join me in the adventure into the unknown.

Come discover new solutions. Check out new pathways with me. My spiritual name is Pathfinder. I know how to achieve, in spades. I also know how to hang out in the space in between. I don't know how to write this book. That is part of the adventure. This is not a project from A to Z. It's a journey into the unknown, the space in between Z and A.

Tag along with me as we cross the chasm of no data. Come fly with me as we follow the flight of intuition. Then we can chart it. But first we have to experience it.

# The Writing Begins

They say there is a book in everyone. Perhaps that's true. Whether you dream of writing a best seller, a blog or just for fun, you have to take that first step. Every writer has their own way of doing things. My approach is that writing involves everything. In order to write I surrender to the natural flow of energy, whether it be emotions, thoughts, moving my body, listening to Spirit in meditation or painting intuitively. I weave in exercises from mind, body and spirit as I go along.

Every one of my books has had a life of its own. The process for one does not get repeated for the next one. Every book project is like a treasure hunt. I don't know what I will discover along the way or where my writing will take me. I like that. It appeals to the explorer in me. Seldom do I write in a linear fashion.

Every writing project has had a challenge for me. This time it's a nervousness of putting the text out there as I go along, blogging it post by post. A skittishness in staying connected to my own guidance as the comments roll in. I didn't show my first book to anyone until I felt it was done. Then I asked my hand picked readers to tell me gently if they thought it was crap. Some like straight on criticism, I prefer to be handled with care.

This time the writing is on the space in between. Magic space. Going from Z to A. It needs a different approach. I need to explain the intangible somehow, using my own life as an example. I've found that sharing my stories make the concepts come alive. It no longer is just a dry metaphysical idea, out there somewhere. You get to experience it live, in action. You get a real life illustration. This book has taken some time to come together. It's been written in the spaces in between. How appropriate!

My life has had a number of interruptions, so the material has come in bits and pieces. The chapters are not in chronological order, but rather sorted by ponderings in the moment. You will notice that a lot of my confusion in this space has centered around where I'm meant to be geographically. Your process will be different. Your questions will be different. Your Z 2 A may be about a deeper understanding of the creative process, or about healing, or an aha in the moment. Simply let my meanderings assist you in exploring your own space in between.

To further deepen the experience, I have chosen to illustrate this book with my own art. The images are there to assist your mind to access Z 2 A space and time. Breathing spaces for your mind so to speak. Let time stand still while you ponder the paintings. Let your eyes rest, let them float through the art. Allow yourself to be swept away on a 'walkabout' of the mind. The longer you meditate on a painting, the more you will see. All of a sudden, it comes alive. What you see is yours to see. Some people experience my art as healing. Some see joy, where others see pain. Some become fascinated with what the image represents. What makes intuitive art so exciting, is that you can get ten different interpretations from ten different people. Try turning the images and discover something new when it's upside down, or on its side.

In the west we know how to do A to Z. We know how to be goal oriented, productive, efficient and focused. There are tons of books on the subject 'how to manage' your project, career, life or whatever from A to Z.

What we lack are instructions how to negotiate, navigate or be in that space in between. I've tried to fill that gap.

# My Plans Were

I had written three books in a row, with little time in between to allow for any serious marketing endeavors. Finally it was time to hit the road and peddle my wares. The European tour would encompass ten countries and 14 thousand kilometers of driving. I had arranged to do *Eva Parties* at American and Swedish organizations all around Europe. You know, instead of Tupperware, you get Eva and her books, live and in the moment.

When I meditated on the overall marketing plan, it felt like I would do Europe first, come home for a couple of months, then tour North America and the British Isles in a series of trips.

The European tour came off as planned. It was a great success, and I felt a renewed sense of being in the flow. When I came home I started to realize that my path forward may not turn out as I had planned.

I had been on the road for two and a half months. I had met lots of people, done many presentations, seen much of Europe, spoken a variety of languages, gotten a lot of feedback as well as new input and sold a lot of books. I needed to rest.

As my life now is about following my inner guidance and learning more and more to be present in the moment, I let myself land gently.

I unpacked the car, did the laundry, cleaned house, restocked the fridge and freezer, developed the pictures I'd taken and put them in albums, sorted papers, read the mail, paid bills and caught up on my email correspondence. I saw my friends, reconnecting and establishing our relationships anew, sometimes in a renewed way. I'd changed and so had they. It's not automatic that you pick up where you left off. I sent thank you notes to all the people I'd visited, bringing closure to the trip. I slept a lot and read a lot. I spent time just being, sitting on the couch staring into space or stretched out and daydreaming.

- What are you working on now? people wondered.
- I'm in the space in between, I'd respond.
- What do you mean?
- Oh, it's that space after one phase is completed and before the next one starts, I'd reply.
- But what are your plans after this? they'd insist.
- My plans were to take off on another tour, but right now I'm landing from the last one, just letting myself be in that space in between. I need to be in the now and let whatever is meant to happen unfold. I don't need to know yet what is next. First I just need to land.

We've become so accustomed to always knowing what our plans are, to have schedules set, to be in charge of our lives. This can lead us to miss a fantastic opportunity. As I was landing from my trip, I kept talking about the space in between. I kept emphasizing the need for me to rest in the moment, that when I had done that, the next step would become clear. There is no sense in rushing forward with plans just because you said earlier you'd do them. The energy has to feel right.

A short time before coming home I'd received an email from a spiritual teacher that I'm sure planted a seed:

Hi all! We have decided to skip November's call for a variety of arcane to mundane reasons and ALSO encourage you all to skip something you have committed yourself to do! It is, of course, terribly forbidden and, therefore, quite delicious!

Giving ourselves permission to beg out on a commitment. There is tremendous freedom in this. The message encouraged me to review my plans. To stay open to the messages and possibilities present in this moment.

Some of the time my energy was lethargic. I felt like I could hibernate on the couch forever. A sense of deep boredom would overwhelm me, then restlessness would make me fidgety and itchy. It's like my body and energy were still moving and hadn't caught up with the fact that we were home. Some part of me was still revved up in action mode, with a green light of GO! But in reality I had before me a red STOP!

When we've been accustomed to constant achievement and it suddenly stops, we can feel very uncomfortable. The routine of being constantly occupied is reassuring. We know it. The space in between isn't comfortable. Most of us experience unease and unrest, sometimes it gets downright chaotic. If we have any unresolved issues or patterns, this is usually when they pop up. A positive achievement is strengthening to the system, builds up good energy as it were, so that another layer can be peeled off the onion. It happened to me this time. I was on a high. Life was great, I'd been on a forward wave, on a roll.

I DON'T NEED TO KNOW YET WHAT IS NEXT

# Then Comes a Receding Wave

Nature shows the way. Like the waves of the ocean, after a forward wave comes a receding wave. It felt like a backlash. I'd had so much forward and positive momentum. Circumstances beyond my control altered my plans. But, come to think of it, when do we ever have control over circumstances?

Right before I left on the European tour, my parents moved back to Sweden, after 38 years in the United States. I'd made the move back myself seven years earlier. By now I'd built up a whole new life for myself. There are no relatives in my vicinity, so my circle of friends only include those I've chosen to be my family. It used to be my mother who would insist on frequent family gatherings. As a single person I found it difficult at times to have enough time for a life of my own.

With my parents move to Sweden, it's all of a sudden my father who becomes the challenge. He calls me while I'm traveling and leaves several messages before I even get home. It's like he doesn't want to understand that I am busy and working and not available. I send as many postcards as I can, but there is very little time to communicate with anyone. Even my closest friend has to make do with sporadic text messages.

Back home, my father keeps calling.

- When are you coming? We could use your help.

OK, intellectually I understand that with age, people lose touch with reality and boundaries, that their grip on functioning in the world slips away. In many ways, they become like children, but with a grown-ups sense of identity.

### RIDE THE WAVE

My mother, although she is drifting deeper into dementia, understands perfectly well my need to land and unwind.

When I finally go visit them for three days, I help them with some things that it didn't take my particular skills to do. In a way it's more difficult for me. I don't know the stores and businesses in town, so I'm at a loss where to turn.

My father's demanding ways feel suffocating to me. I find it really hard to understand why he would decline help from those who want to help him, and insist that I be the one to take care of it all.

I'd had a space of seven years without their presence. When they tried to step into it again, it became crystal clear how much space that was. Yet another reason the space in between is so important. Without it we wouldn't understand how we've grown. It's in the meantime that the change happens.

As Winter Solstice approached, the real New Year as far as I am concerned, I started to make a wish list. Lots of new ideas were percolating. I let myself be open to new and different projects for the new year.

Making lists, drawing mind maps, making collages of our desires are one way to work with the possibilities in the ethers. Z 2 A phases present us with a myriad of options. By pulling them in, closer to the physical plane, we stir the pot.

I'll include my wish list here along with my questions and reflections, so you can take part in my process of unfolding in the space in between. Clearly lots of ideas as well as confusion. Be inspired to make your own list, full of inconsistencies and unrealistic expectations. Dare to dream. Vocalize your inner wishes. Listen to your heart. Let your mind soar on the winds of change.

## Wish List for 2006

- lots of love
- a man who gives me what I need
- an overflowing income
- good relationships
- happiness and success
- to enjoy life, pleasure

– to feel safe

## Possible Trips

- USA tour, appear on Oprah
- British Isles tour, London Book Fair, EU Michael Retreat
- tour Asia & Australia
- Corsica
- Loire Valley

## Possible Courses

- A Book is Born
- Life Therapy leadership training in Sweden
- Dance of Life in Swedish and/or English
- Dance as a Therapeutic Tool
- The Creative Living Seminar - five days in the flow

## Possible Book Projects

- A Book is Born
- A New Dawn
- Nomad
- Life is a Pleasure Hunt
- Spa Healing Temple
- Series Life Therapy books
- The Space in Between
- Empowerment - Discover a different way of life - Dance of Life
- Immigrant in my own country
- Books in Swedish
- Do audio books

## Reflections and questions

- Where is the energy and enthusiasm?
- Which activities lead to the fulfillment of my wishes at the top of the list?
- Again the question of working in Swedish or English? Live here, customers there? Need to end the question
- AND, not OR

- You have an absolute best seller within you (says a psychic friend of mine)
- go job hunting locally?

As the wish list unfolded, expanded and refined, I sensed something else coming down the pike. The trick is to let the uncertainty be there, the not knowing what is to unfold. To ride the wave of chaos, to be in the stillness, to hang out in the creative void until the fog lifts. To allow the confusion to be there in the meantime.

# The Michael Teachings

Throughout this book I refer to the Michael Teachings. I first came across the writings of Chelsea Quinn Yarbro in the early 1980's. My friends and I read and discussed the *Messages from Michael* trilogy of books. As more books arrived, we read them too. Here were matters we'd all thought about, but hadn't quite found the words to express what we knew, somewhere inside. Reading and discussing brought clarity, then more questions, all the while deepening our understanding of why we are here.

THE MICHAELS EXPLAIN THE DEEPER SIDE OF LIFE

Michael is a group soul that channels through many individuals messages about why we are here. They explain how the soul journeys from the Tao and back. The teachings cover soul age, role, attitudes, modes, agreements and tasks. They talk a lot about choice. And much much more.

It's the deep philosophy of life that so strongly attracts me to the Michael teachings. Understanding how we form agreements and why, before we ever incarnate on earth. How we create and heal karmic knots. The roles we take on with each other, helping each other grow, in lifetime after lifetime.

The Michael Teachings web site is an excellent source for further study.

# Playing with Titles and Subtitles

While a book is coming together, it may start out with a working title, or idea, then go through permutations before arriving at the published title. Partly this is caused by a book not being set in concrete before it is written. I may start out with a thread or theme, and as the writing progresses that theme may expand, change or move into a whole new direction. So playing with titles and subtitles as you go along is another part of the writing process. It also helps to focus awareness on 'what is the essence of this book?'

Your process may be about something else entirely, but you can use the titles and subtitles idea to stir your own pot. As you explore one idea, something else pops up. It's a journey, an exploration of bits and pieces, that may not seem related, at this time. Use my process to inspire yours.

### So far, nominations for titles and subtitles are

- From Z to A - navigating the space in between (or trusting the space in between?)
- Slow Motion Enlightenment
- Trusting the Now
- Dance in the Flow of Life
- Do the Experience and Trust the Universe
- Expand Your Thinking
- Crossing the Chasm of No Data
- Lost in Space
- Void Voyager

PLAYING WITH POSSIBILITIES IS ONE WAY TO LET THE
VARIOUS PATHWAYS COME TO THE SURFACE. MAKE
A LIST. THEN LET IT BE. SET IT TO RISE LIKE A GOOD
DOUGH.

I also like to work on the layout while shaping the book.
Fonts, headings, line spacings and margins all affect the feel
of the book and to my way of thinking need to reflect the soul
of the writing. It all has to be consistent. But like life, you never know where the journey is going to take you until you start
to travel.

Your process may have nothing to do with writing a book.
But wherever you find yourself in life, when you're not sure
where you're going, playing with possibilities is one way to let
the various pathways come to the surface. Make a list. Then
let it be. Set it to rise like a good dough.

# When in the Fog Stand Still

The Buddhists say

WHEN IN THE FOG STAND STILL

Which at first glance could be interpreted to do nothing. Not at all. The standing still refers to being totally present in the process, wherever it takes you. It means surrendering at the deepest level. Letting go of ego and mind of how it should look or about what makes sense.

SOMETHING ELSE WANTED TO HAPPEN, BUT WHAT?

You can see from my questions in the chapter *Then comes*

*a receding wave* that I try to make sense of the fact that I live in Sweden yet seem destined to write in English. Well it's true so far, but one doesn't preclude the other. I need to let myself be open to be guided to what is on the path for me now, in this moment. To let myself follow the energy as it unfolds. It may not make much sense in the moment, but I can't see as far as my guidance. I am not privy to the whole picture down here. I trust that I am guided for my highest good.

Of course, when in the fog, standing still may be the most appropriate action, or non action as it were.

It so happens, while I was hanging out in the void, between the end of my European tour and the beginning of 'what next?' this book began to take shape. I just allowed myself to be in the fog, write wish lists, drink lots of tea while watching the snow flakes fall, listening to the silence of winter. Instead of any planned book project, this one wanted to be born. It's all about be here now and let the future unfold.

You may notice that the space in time I am referring to was some time ago. What happened? I wrote quite a bit on this book and felt lots of excitement as ideas percolated and surfaced, bubbling like a brook in Spring. I had written about 20 thousand words, when the writing skidded to a halt. Something else wanted to happen, but what?

Confusion, or fog, rolled in. Resistance to a change of direction. I wanted to write my Z 2 A book - NOW! You know how it is

I HAD A PLAN
TURNED OUT GOD HAD ANOTHER PLAN
GUESS WHO WAS RIGHT?

Yep, I needed to alter my plans, again. But I didn't acquiesce easily.

# What You Resist Persists

Resistance, is mostly the ego trying to maintain control, insisting on my way or the highway. It's seldom a successful strategy. Eventually we realize that the universe knows best. So,

### WHAT YOU RESIST PERSISTS

until you get it. The God force or your Higher Self doesn't care how many times it has to show you the way. They want what is best for us. But trusting and letting go doesn't come easy to a human. Especially those of us brought up in the West to rely on logic and intellectual structure and plans, like bulleted lists. Useful at times, but not when you want to flow in the spiritual river of life and creation.

### I REMEMBER TO SURRENDER

was the mantra that came to me while I was undergoing Re-birthing Therapy a number of years ago. Off and on I'm reminded to surrender. When my plan doesn't seem to be going anywhere. When my path forward gets blocked. When the energy fizzles for what I thought I was meant to be doing. That's what happened to this book. I got quite a ways into it, and it skidded to a halt.

So what happened in between? After all, this is a book about that space and time. The energy went dead for the Z 2 A book project. No trips were on the horizon. I'm in stay at home mode. Even a Sagittarian needs to let her suitcase gather dust once in a while.

My Swedish friends kept prodding me about a book in Swedish. To be honest, it was not what I wanted to do. But, right before I had left on that European tour, I'd gotten the same question. Over and over.

- Why don't you write a book in Swedish?

Their questions set me off, pissed me off if I were to be honest. 'I'll show you, I have lots to say if I were to write in Swedish,' I thought. And proceeded to write the outline of a book, in Swedish, in just a few days. Then I went off on my trip and forgot about it. Only to have it resurface as my resistance was at its peak.

BE INSPIRED TO QUIT RESISTING

I was surprised to see how much I had written at the peak

of my emotional intensity. There was more than enough for a book there. All I had to do was write it. I still wasn't convinced.

The summer before I had spent an evening with friends. The question of writing in Swedish had surfaced then too, but a much bigger subject had been audio books. Yes, I had thought the thought. But when my gaggle of friends kept insisting in unison 'you have a wonderful voice, you ought to make audio books,' I had to agree.

As with many things, the seeds get sown long before they start to sprout. They lay dormant until it's time to help them grow into maturity.

I did some research on audio books. How to record one? How do I distribute it? How would I do it? It was a good excuse to get a new computer, with recording capability. With a little help from the Apple Discussion Forum I was set to start. My first test was reading one of my already published books. It felt unnatural and the energy just didn't feel right. Then during one of my walks the penny dropped. I'll do it like I do all my talks and courses, live and in the moment.

I was energized. I knew I was on the right track. As part of my research I had learned that Sweden, along with Germany, were at the leading edge of the distribution of audio books on the Internet. That tipped the scales, I would do an audio book in Swedish.

Like a steam train pulling out of a station, it was slow and not without friction at the start. I felt ridiculous sitting in front of a microphone. I started with gibberish. Make noise, keep the vocal going, many starts, but after a few hours it felt like I had primed the pump and was ready to record. I did the whole book in a week. Seven hours of *Eva Live and in the Moment*. An extended Eva Party.

I don't know if anyone else has gone straight to digital, normally you write the book first. It was novel enough to get me written up in the papers and interviewed on the radio. You may notice I digress, might as well get used to it. My style is meandering. If you think of it like you are sitting beside me in the sofa and we are sharing tea while our conversation meanders.

Resistance comes in many flavors. There's denial, where you keep insisting that it's not your job. All the while the universe is bugging you, with questions from friends, or proddings from newspapers and television. Everywhere you look, there it is. The thing you don't want to do. But you keep denying you are to have any part in it.

Then there's the 'I don't want' tactic. Like me. Very grown up. More like a petulant child, who keeps saying no. Digging my heels in. I don't want to do this. OK, but why not take all that against energy and turn it into for energy. Let it become fore like in golf. Use the resistance and turn it into 'I'll show you.' Unleash the powers that reside within you. There's no need to be elegant about it. Bring all your pesky emotions with you. Use that emotional force to do the thing that is before you. You'll be amazed at how productive that steam locomotive called 'I don't want' can be.

Distractions are another great tactic to avoid that thing that has your name on it. Playing games on social media sites, chatting with friends, running from one activity to the next or filling up the social calendar. Checking the refrigerator. You become busy with other stuff. But the universe keeps persisting.

I quit resisting and unleashed a flurry of creative energy. Not to mention that I improved my cash flow. My audio book hit the top ten chart for library loans the first week. So be inspired to quit resisting, there can be gold at the end of that rainbow, but you'll never find out if you keep resisting. And as long as you resist, it persists, until you let go and surrender. So what are you waiting for? Someone to push you off the cliff, so you can discover that you indeed could fly?

# Uncorked

Turns out the audio book was just the beginning. My energy was really flowing now. But, I had to work myself through the resistance. It wasn't easy. I wanted to get back to this, my Z 2 A project. I still didn't want to write that book in Swedish. Eventually I relented. I quit being stubborn, and with lots of grumbling and emotional intensity I dug out my Swedish book writing project.

Surrendering does not have to be elegant. Surrendering does not necessarily mean you do it with joy. Surrendering can let loose a flurry of emotion. At times it's the best therapy. So just let it rip.

That's what I proceeded to do. I took the rough draft and started expanding on it. In between I painted, danced, emoted, cried, laughed, swore, and got high on the creative energy. I spent hours talking to my friends, discussing, chewing on principles, trying to understand, turning over lots of issues and ideas.

Uncorking the flow lets the champagne bubble up. I'm not saying it's an easy or smooth journey, but in the end you can see some amazing results. During summer, I was a long ways into the draft, a rough one mind you, and people kept asking when they could read it. I did something I had never done before. I let it out of my hands before censoring anything. It was a rough draft alright, with all my grumblings and acerbic comments left in. It didn't sit well with some people, but some very fruitful dialogue came out of it. The polished and finished book was a much improved animal published as *The Courage to Live*. The path is rarely straight.

**UNCORKING THE FLOW
LETS THE CHAMPAGNE BUBBLE UP**

# Not Enough Space?

At times it feels like there is not enough space for me. The agendas of other people push on my envelope. Where does the need come from to meddle in another person's affairs? I reflect on this in dealing with my ageing parents. Looking at my need to create order in their life. I realized I can't impose my standard on how much clutter one should live with on them. I need to respect their integrity. They have chosen to hang out on earth to learn certain lessons. I can't, and shouldn't, take that away from them.

Outer clutter is merely a reflection of inner clutter. There's a comfort level with the amount of space around us. Look at how a person who loves to live in the woods might feel uncomfortable with the wide open spaces of the prairie, or the vastness of the ocean. On the other hand, those who breathe deeply with wide open spaces often feel claustrophobic in the middle of the forest, or in a basin surrounded by mountains.

How much stuff is your comfort zone? How much furniture feels comfortable in a room? How many pictures hanging on the wall? To one person bright, intense colors are a comfort, whereas the next person is soothed by warm pastels, or pale icy shades. Just think about the number of plants in a room that make your soul soar with happiness.

When other people bombard me with their solution, I feel like I don't have enough space. At times I feel like I can't breathe. I have to remind myself that I am the pilot of my life.

I make the decisions and prioritize what I need to make it work for me.

IT'S UP TO US TO SEE BEYOND THE VEIL

What good would it do me to wake up at the end of my life, only to discover I had been living someone else's idea of it? Hopefully I'd learn to make different choices in the next life. But there is no time like the present.

Life presents us with opportunities for learning, all the time. The rest periods where you can just glide along, sail on smooth water, do come in between. Then comes a new challenge. That is the ebb and flow of life. I've often reflected on how the universe calls on me to be present and truly reflect on what is mine to do. How do I feel now, rather than respond by rote, this is how it is.

When we are Z 2 A, suggestions come from all around us. It's up to us to see beyond the veil.

# Hanging Loose in Networks

Over the years, I've participated in a number of groups and networks. What starts out with a few people wanting to get together to share and exchange information can soon turn into a formal something with rules and regulations.

While I was active as a therapist, a local network was started. I joined in and helped recruit others. The idea being to meet once in a while to exchange information, discuss experiences, support each other, trade sessions and not least of all get some social time. Very soon, someone in the group wanted to formalize the network, draw up organization bylaws and elect officers. My enthusiasm faded in a jiffy. All of a sudden the focus had shifted from the connecting aspect to a formal 1-2-3 box.

The minute you impose rigid standards of meetings and minutes, you take away a lot of the creative aspect of a lateral network. Sure enough, half the members dropped out and eventually the group 'died' from lack of oxygen.

As a writer I was invited to join another network. They guy who started it intended it to be a social get together when the spirit moved us at the local coffee shop. I specifically asked if he wanted to make a formal club or seek grants and such.

- Absolutely not, he said.
- Great, I'm in! I replied.

It didn't take long. At the second meeting someone in need of controlling things started pushing for a club with officers, a project to seek grant money was proposed, and half the people left. Again, most people were interested in the connecting and sharing aspect. Many writers are pretty independent types and have had it up to here with rules and regulations.

IN THAT SPACE OF NO CONTROL,
MAGIC COULD HAPPEN

Is it discomfort of loose connections that scare people? And why is it that the controlling types take over? Those of us who don't care about bylaws and dues just slide out the door, and seek connections in other ways. My opinion, perhaps you could say it is my truth with a capital T, is that networks lose a lot when not allowed leeway and looseness. I suppose it ties in with my belief that creative processes and free thinking is hampered by too much formality.

Let go of needing to steer life and its processes. Learn to trust that even without formal bylaws and officers we can have networks that are productive and fun. You never know, in that space of no control, magic could happen. Why not let it in?

# Missing a Piece of the Puzzle

I sent out a spontaneous email to my Swedish list. Normally, my messages are quite businesslike and focused on marketing. This one was different, driven by some inner inspiration. It came together with ease. I just sat down and wrote it, sent it off, with a very OK feeling about my inconsistent wishes. I had no idea I would get such response. As the process lurched along and memories, connections, insights and help rolled in I realized I needed to include it in this book. So bear with me as I tell you stories and paths that now seem to be coming full circle, all the while journeying with me in the space in between. I like to think of it as applied spirituality. Perhaps the best way to illustrate something is to make it come alive,

But first, let me translate the Swedish email, titled

## Missing a piece of the puzzle

This July/August I travel to the United States, my other home country. Booked in Seattle, Mountain View and Sacramento and invited to Denver/Boulder County and San Diego/Fallbrook. But it feels like there is a piece of the puzzle missing. This year seems to be a year of movement for many, and I must admit the nomad in me is feeling restless. Three years ago I let go of Paradise and did a 'walkabout' in Europe by car that eventually landed me back in Eksjö, this time in town. I was fully aware then that this apartment was a stopover, a good base for all the trips I was going to take to market my books.

But I feel the time is approaching to move again. But where?

I long for a climate where you can be outdoors for most of the year, without freezing your keister off. On the other hand, I like contrasts. I long for the sea, to wander along sandy beaches that stretch for miles... on the other hand I like leafy forests and meadows, but it needs to be open landscapes, where I can breathe, fill my lungs with air. Where I can gaze across the wide open spaces. To watch the snowflakes descend in silence with a pot of tea and good conversation is also alright. Water is a must, sea, lake, babbling brook, a slow river...

I want to live in a place where there is a demand for my services, where it goes without saying that my seminars are appreciated and in demand. Where it is easy to connect and create networks, where the social life is easy and natural. Where I feel at home and won't have to listen to comments like 'I don't imagine you'll end up staying here...'

Those of you who have listened to and read my Swedish books *Eva Live and in the Moment* and *The Courage to Live* know why and how I happened to land in Paradise and Eksjö and also know that this work is complete. But what is next? The United States again? Or? My feeling is that all these trips are for the purpose of finding the new, contacts, contexts, seminar possibilities and all that surrounds a whole life.

If thoughts appear spontaneously as you read this, let me know...

I felt excitement as I hit the send button. Then I settled into the day and the insights rolled in with an emotional intensity I could not have predicted.

# Insight Rolls In

As I settled into my morning meditation, I noticed a lot of energy right away, as a result of sending out the missing puzzle piece email. I felt free and happy to have written something personal. For once it wasn't about promoting my stuff in a 'business like' fashion, it was just a note about my feelings, in the moment. I became aware of a weariness of *breathing out*, which is how I think of marketing. Sometimes I feel like I'm shouting into empty space. I'm sensing its high time for *breathing in*, which is how I think of much of my creative stuff and to get on with the writing of this book.

Relaxing into my meditation, there was emotion. Relief, some quiet tears. A wondering what I was still doing here in Sweden? When I had taken off from Paradise three years ago, I was heading for Annecy in France with certainty and strong guidance. The weird thing is, I felt the shift on the way down. Somewhere in Germany, I felt that someone had changed their mind, that a definite shift had happened. It felt like a rubber band pulling me back. I didn't understand it then, but as I journeyed on it was clear as a bell I did not belong in Annecy. I had a few more things to sort out and experience, so I didn't go back straight away. As I continued my 'walkabout' by car, the connection to my friends in Sweden became very strong. I realized that for the next few years, I would be taking off on tours to market my books, so I needed a base. Logic prevailed and I headed back to Sweden. I also knew that if I was to change countries, I wanted to be in an English speaking one, and the one that came to mind was the USA.

MEDITATION BRINGS INSIGHT

Back 'home' I spent a fair amount of time settling in before a tour came about, then there was a long space in between and it's only since last fall that I've been going on jaunts, however they haven't been as long as I'd thought. The two trips so far have been to the US.

So instead of having a base to travel from, it felt like I had a base that I was mostly living in. During this time period my parents moved back to Sweden, and to put it mildly, there have been a lot of details to help them with. I'm not your cookies and milk type, or the kind that fluffs your pillows, but they have enough friends and relatives that provide that for them. What I've focused on is helping Dad get all the financial and legal stuff up to snuff, making sure they have the services they need, you know all that structural and organizational stuff, which I happen to be quite good at.

As I sat in meditation, I realized that my job, the big reason I was pulled back to Sweden, was for the purpose of helping my parents settle in. What I had experienced, was their decision on the inner planes to come back here, and that is what pulled me back from moving to France, like a rubber band. It's what kept me here, instead of taking the move directly to the somewhere else. So why did this realization finally hit?

The day before I had met with the social services to start the process to get my parents into assisted living. I figured it might take a long time before my Mother would see it that way, and I was totally floored when she was on the same page from the get go. She turns to my Dad and says 'I think it's a good idea, to move into a place where there is full service.' As it is, the home service in Sweden works very well, but there is a limit to what they can provide. We're close to maxed out with them.

What I had been waiting for, energetically, was to understand why I was needed back in Sweden. The emotions that came roaring in during the day were very strong. Mostly a lot of crying of relief. Understanding. It's not like I've sat and rolled my thumbs. Moving retired people with ailments, dual citizenship, bank accounts in several places, well you can imagine all the stuff that needed to be sorted and simplified. Not to mention sorting out undocumented loans and wills. But I've taken it one step at a time.

It feels like this thing with my parents is an agreement

that we have. Not like karma, but agreement, where you take on a specific task to assist another soul (or fragment, as the Michaels like to call us). When the agreement is understood, there is often intense emotional relief, as the insight floods in why you have felt so compelled to hang in there. The funny thing is, while you are doing the agreement, you don't know it. It's only when it is revealed that you see the whole thread. I suppose we are not meant to know ahead of time, as we always have choice. It is not cast in concrete that either of us will complete the agreement. A fragment can abdicate an agreement, which does have consequences and emotional fallout.

In my book *Secrets of Transformation* I tell the story of my twin sister, who abdicated the agreement to be my sister three months into the womb. Unraveling the knots and setting each other free took some time, but once I was willing to see my part, it went a lot easier. There is an amazing amount of energy tied up in unresolved abdicated agreements.

So why didn't I know sooner that I had and agreement to help my parents resettle in Sweden? Probably because it would have interfered with the work, or lessons to be learned. It's as if a veil is put between you and the threads, to keep you plugging along. If you knew at the get go that you were completing an agreement, you may forgo other experiences in your life. The risk would be that you'd approach it from a let's get this done and over with, or maybe you'd over focus on the agreement and miss other aspects. I can only say that knowing about it ahead of time would not have served me.

This wasn't the completion of my agreement with my parents. I'm still helping them out. So be careful of the conclusions you draw. I was given the insight I had an agreement to help them at the time I needed it most, not when we were done. It's very easy to misinterpret signals in life. It's very easy to interpret understanding as completion. It's very easy to interpret a no as a definite not at all, instead of a not now at this moment no.

# In the Meantime

While I've been back in Sweden 'waiting' to complete this agreement with my parents, I haven't been idle. When I returned, sans furniture or place to live, a friend called and said 'why don't you land here with us, we have plenty of room.' I ended up staying for two months until I could move into my new apartment in town. My friends live in the country, in the woods with several kilometers to the nearest neighbor.

While I was there, the biggest storm in Swedish history hit, felling five years worth of trees in one night. We were without power or phone the last three weeks of my stay. Talk about going into the void, the space in between, hibernation, getting back to basics. We were lucky. They had kept the wood stove in the kitchen so we could cook and stay warm. They had kept the well so we could fetch fresh water. The outhouse was still there, complete with a Styrofoam seat. If you haven't done the outhouse experience in the midst of winter, imagine sitting down on freezing wood. Now imagine parking your rear on Styrofoam. It makes a world of difference. Makes you appreciate the little things.

We spent a lot of time drinking tea and talking. There wasn't much else you could do. It was a fantastic interlude, a period of shutting off the world. Attitude makes such a difference. If you accept what is and adjust, life becomes ever so much easier.

I had a great time moving into my apartment. Starting over from scratch with furnishings to suit who I'd become, at that moment. The apartment is only 500 square feet, but very well laid out. Between IKEA, second hand shops and hand me downs from my friends, I did really well. It dawned on me that it was cheaper to start over than moving all your belongings. Now isn't that interesting? Makes it kind of fun. You can begin totally anew, each time you move, if you so choose.

IN THE MEANTIME

Settling in, decorating, buying plants, hanging out with friends, I started planning trips. That fall I took off on the pan European tour of ten countries. On my return, landing in the space in between, the idea for this book started to take shape. But it wasn't time for it quite yet.

# Magic Hour?

I don't know how many times I've been up at 4 o'clock in the morning to write. It's like someone wakes me up and the ideas are there, clear and ready to put down. Now I know I'm not alone. When I watched the movie *Conversations with God*, which portrays the story of how the books by the same name came into being, I had to laugh. Over and over, at 4 am, Neale Donald Walsch is awakened, to write down the answers to all the questions he's been asking God.

Is 4 am the magic hour for writers? Perhaps. I do know it's quiet on the airwaves. There is a similar feeling on weekends, there is less interference in the ethers.

My writing often comes in surges. There is a flurry of ideas that need to be captured, I have lots of energy. I'm wide awake at 4 o'clock in the morning and sharp as can be. When I'm in not writing mode, wild horses couldn't get me out of bed before 8 or 9. Then I can sleep, a lot. This seems to be true of creative types. The need for sleep varies enormously.

# Imagine my Surprise

Imagine my surprise when my inbox filled up with responses to my puzzle piece email. Normally, I get a few replies, but this time all kinds of spontaneous answers popped in:
- an inquiry to take over my apartment
- a suggestion that I'm done with what I've been doing and perhaps it was time to return to the corporate world
- a recognition of synchronicity that big change is in the air, she was about to change careers and country
- observation my wishes are inconsistent and perhaps the solution would be found in staying; it takes time to build a new life and business
- several suggestions that France would resonate with me
- a couple of questions what happened to the idea of Tenerife
- recognition I was in a state of change with a lead for a great psychic/channel to consult
- comment I was at a crossroads with an offer of a free half hour of coaching
- information from two major retreat centers that would like my business
- reflections from quite a few of their own change plans or dreams
- lovely pictures of the setting sun over water
- a suggestion to check out a coastal area in the south of Sweden
- a vision of me in coastal France, Spain or California

- an update from a kindred spirit who also longs for the wide open spaces and water
- an invitation to a Creative Dance event
- some feedback that what I was describing sounded very much like where I was living

Naturally, all this feedback, questions and ideas helped me to go deeper into my own process. Memories resurfaced as I talked to friends or responded to the emails, helping to clarify my path forward. It's like I went on a closet cleaning of the mind, letting go of that which no longer fit me. An update to who I am today.

All the while keeping in mind that other people's reflections were their view of what I was saying, their perception of who I am and where I might need to go. One person quipped she would get confused by all this input. Well, I've had some practice to sort what is mine and what is yours. If you've ever overdone the 'go ask a psychic routine' when your intuition already has given you the answers, you know what I'm talking about. You get so many conflicting views on who you are, that you end up totally confused. Which is not necessarily a bad place to be. With confusion overload, the mental fences are harder to keep intact. Perhaps allowing the unexpected to enter.

# Blue Notes

Whilst on a painting retreat, we spent an evening listening to blues and light jazz. One number they introduced as Blue Notes, named for all the half notes used to create the blues. They use the notes in between. Perfect for Z 2 A.

# Annecy, France

Midsummer 2004 in Paradise, Sweden

I stirred gently. The morning breeze caressed my face as the birds were singing in the trees outside my window. As I slowly drifted awake the thought came to me clear as a bell. Today is the day to give notice on this house. It's time to move.

I'd been in this rental house six years. Since the beginning of June I'd had a sense that I'd be moving in September. I kept asking my inner guidance if I shouldn't give notice, seeing as it's three months notice and if I'm to move in September that means now. I'd been thinking that to move in September meant the 1st. As my thoughts cleared on this midsummer morning, I realized they had meant for me to move at the end of September. Now it all made sense. It always does in the end. We just have to stay patient and trust the guidance and the process. My logical mind isn't always too happy with this, but over the years it's had to acquiesce that the guidance always works out.

My inner guidance, intuition, higher self, God, whatever you want to call it, has greater vision than I do. It can see around the bend where the logical mind can't reach. It knows it's not always wise to make me privy to why I'm guided to certain actions, because if I don't know ahead of time what I'm in for, I'll do the experience and learn what I need to learn. If I was given the whole plan ahead of time, it would spoil the process, the actual going through it. I mean, would you really want to know everything that was to happen to you in your life? How much fun would that be? Would you really live if you knew? The guidance helps us move forward, but we have to do the experience. That's what enriches us.

So I sent off an email to my landlady, that I would be moving at the end of September. At this time I did not know where I was moving to. All I had a sense of was that it was somewhere further south in Europe, perhaps Switzerland or France, but not really sure. I was guided to sell off everything and pack up the car and head out. Quite an adventure. For some reason it didn't scare me. I'd already experienced taking off with only the clothes on my back when I left my ex-husband, and learned that life goes on and that my possessions aren't me. It was actually a very freeing experience.

I would be lying if I said I was totally comfortable with not knowing where I was going. I was hoping I'd be given a destination before it was time to head out and not have to rely on a sense, stop here and settle. That was too unsettling, even for me. But as I'd given notice on the house, I started to tell my friends I would be moving at the end of September.

First reactions were we must get together before you go. Some experienced a sadness. Now that we'd made friends they were sad to see me go. Others realized how close we had become. If I hadn't been moving, that realization may not have dropped in. So the summer became one of many outings and get togethers, discourses on how we'd met and how our friendships had developed. What it was like when I had first arrived. How we'd met and where. It was as if by me moving, lots of feelings and recognitions surfaced. For me as well, I realized how well I had done my work of building an emotional support network.

My landlady came to visit. In the course of conversation she asked where I was moving.

- Somewhere near Switzerland it feels like, most likely the French part, I say.

- That's close to Annecy, the most beautiful place in the world I've ever been to, says my landlady.

Quite a statement from her as she has traveled a lot and seen many wonderful places. We get the map out and she shows me where it is, not far across the border into France, a little south of Geneva. We get onto talking about other things and I don't reflect further on Annecy - as yet.

Then it's time for a painting weekend and of course my friends want to know where exactly I'm moving to. I still feel like it's somewhere in the Switzerland region, perhaps Lausanne or somewhere along Lac Leman.

- Where exactly is that? asks Kristina.

- Close to France and the Alps, I reply.

- It was somewhere near there that my husband called me, on the one trip he took without me, says Kristina. The bus had just pulled into town and he just had to call.

- If we ever move anywhere, this is where we'll come, he says. We've just arrived in the most beautiful place in the world, a town called Annecy.

As Kristina is relating this and Annecy pops up again, I think this is too weird.

- That's exactly what my landlady said. Annecy is the most beautiful place in the world, I exclaim.

- Really, what a coincidence, someone else in the group says.

I get a strong feeling this is a message from my guides. Annecy is the place. Switzerland was just to get you in the vicinity, but here is your destination.

I go home and surf the Internet, learn that Annecy is like the Venice of France. It has a lake, mountains, canals and is very charming. OK, I think, Annecy it is. Destination revealed. At ease that I know where to go. I do ponder taking a flight down to do the apartment hunting, but my previous experience of France is that it's relatively easy to find furnished housing. I do contact the tourist office and a number of other agencies and they basically confirm my feeling that it's best to look when I arrive.

I go on about my business, terminating telephone and other

contracts, call the auction firm to arrange to sell my stuff. He says he charges a ten percent commission, at that rate there is no sense in me trying to sell everything through the paper myself. I'll be better off letting them handle it.

I'm relieved and happy to be going back to France. I had secretly hoped I would get to go somewhere I felt at home. I've often said I have a Swedish body, an American mind and a French soul.

The last week or so before I leave, I get yet another letter from the tax authorities. Three years out of six they have hounded me about some idiotic detail, that can't make any difference to their coffers. This time they want to review my bookkeeping. One of the reasons I'm moving is the lack of financial viability of running a therapy business. Although by now I've switched to writing books, which you can do anywhere.

I call up the tax office to explain I'm shutting down my business and moving, so what difference can it make for them to go through all my papers with a fine tooth comb.

- Where are you moving to, she inquires out of curiosity.
- Annecy, in France, I respond.
- Annecy, she exclaims! That is the most beautiful place in the world I've ever been to. I had an incredible spiritual experience while I swam in Lake Annecy.
- Wow, I say. You are the third person to declare Annecy the most beautiful place in the world.

Incredible synchronicity. Third time's a charm. I feel like the universe is making sure I know I'm on the right path. Our messengers do appear in strange places.

# Preparing for Takeoff

Before I left for Annecy I wanted to say farewell to a number of people I may not see for a long time or not at all. I wanted to go up to the north of Sweden and see my relatives and give each one of them a painting. They had helped me so much on my re-entry to Sweden. It is important to bring closure, to end the old, before starting anew.

As I drove north along the coast, I kept having visions of the mountains where both my parents are from. I realized I hadn't been there for 27 years, so I altered my return route and went to see my aunt and cousins there. It was a special trip and special visit. One afternoon my 85 year old aunt and I sat down with a glass of whiskey and pondered life. I felt a strong reconnection to my cousin. When I drove away, I cried. I had no idea why. Last year, that cousin was diagnosed with cancer and died shortly thereafter. Had I picked up on his pending departure on the inner planes?

As you might have gathered by now, I have a lot of aunts. The one in Stockholm is the youngest, we share a love of the color purple. The painting she chose is a whirl of deep blues, purples and silver that now hangs in her elegant bathroom, with towels to match.

Giving away the paintings was part of the preparation process. Letting go made room for new works and energies. One painting went to a soul I've had lots of lives with. At the time, I didn't know of any of our past life connections, that came later. I had to let the painting go, give it away. I was extremely pleased with my work to be sure. But it wasn't for me to keep. The more in tune with the natural energy flow, the easier it is to let go and know when to hang on and when to let go.

Learn to trust the universe. All I need will come to me at the Divine time. All I need to know will be revealed to me at the right moment. When we are who we are supposed to be and doing what we are supposed to do, according to our best understanding of God's will, we are in Grace, we are in flow. If we occupy the space we are truly meant to occupy there is no room for conflict.

It's when we think we should hang onto something which isn't ours, or covet that which truly doesn't belong to us that troubles start. When we refuse to budge from a place we've outgrown, we gum up the works, we contribute to a stagnation of life energy.

The ancient Hawaiians understood life energy. The closest concept they had to sinning was to not follow the path of highest life energy. It's very simple. Follow the path of highest life energy. Do no harm. Carry forgiveness in your heart.

When I took off on my move to what I thought was destination Annecy, I got rid of most of my possessions. It was necessary for me to sell off my old furniture and let go of everything that wasn't to be part of my new life. I couldn't have held onto it. In order for me to move to the next level, I had to step off into the unknown. You can see it as my old possessions and house didn't have the vibration to match me anymore. I was spinning at another frequency. If I had stayed with the old, I would have been stuck and reverted back to my old energy level. This book would not have been possible to write in that space, with those old energies around me.

You have to let go of the old to make room for the new. When I moved into my new apartment, I had lots of fun filling it to suit the new me. My old furniture wouldn't have fit. I would have insisted on a much larger space, but this is exactly what I needed. The creative energy in searching for a couch, for curtains and dishes should not be underestimated. Now my home reflects who I am today. It feels clear of past clutter. Your home is just as important as your garden, as your body, as your car, as your emotional and spiritual self. Their state reflects on who you truly are. They show the world how you feel about yourself. It's easy to drag old stuff along as you move or shift, just out of habit.

Don't.

### YOU HAVE TO LET GO OF THE OLD
### TO MAKE ROOM FOR THE NEW

# Bugs Show the Way to Completion

Many of you are familiar with Totem Animals and their symbolic significance. In Sweden, this has gone a bit further, with books available to understand the meaning of most animals and plants that may cross your path. For some strange reason a couple of Silverfish showed up in my bathroom. Extremely uncommon in this climate, and I can't recall having any in my house since my student days. Well, according to this book, Silverfish represent that there is something you need to complete, let go of. You are hanging on to something that needs to be sorted or rearranged in your life.

It didn't take me long to figure out what. Two things came to mind, of different character, but nonetheless, things to take care of. I had been hanging on to this painting group that meets one weekend a month. For some time, I'd felt a need to move on, to either start my own group, or hang out in a different arrangement, with more freedom to apply other processes in the painting experience. I felt the group more and more was about the social interaction, and less on developing the creative aspect. We all have different needs, and it was clear I was the one with a different viewpoint. The rest of the group are fine with how things are. So I sent a notice I would not be hanging out with them in the fall.

It is so important to tie up loose ends, to finish what is really done. It would not serve me to hang in there, with one foot in waiting for something else to come along. Better to get out of limbo. We need to create space for something better, that is more in tune with who we are at this point.

The other item to complete were pictures. I had almost two years worth of photos waiting to be sorted and put into albums. Now was the time to do that job. I'd finally purchased a digital camera a few weeks earlier. Taking all the paper prints produced with my old camera and throwing away all but the very best and putting them in albums was opportune. We don't get to skip any steps, they are all important!

MAKE A CLEAN SWEEP

Hanging on to people and things that no longer serve us eat up a lot of energy. Leaving projects unfinished zap the life force. Tidying up loose ends help us gain clarity. It's OK to let go.

# Disciples in My Future

With all the inner work I've done over the years, I've gathered quite a toolbox for transition work. I pulled out one of my favorite meditations called *Present - Future.* I asked before going into meditation to see the key to my next place of living. I've observed that it is either a theme or a key that leads us to the next place. It can be a job, a house, a relationship, a sense of community or climate. There is always one theme that stands out more than the rest. That's what I was looking for.

In my future circle I saw a group of disciples, who were eager to learn from me. They are waiting for me to show up. I've long dreamt of having a development group, where I freely get to facilitate the processes and help spur the growth potential of the individuals and the group as a whole. Here it was, wherever I am moving to has this group of people waiting for me. My sense is a group of six to twelve people. A core group in other words.

Next I asked for 'homework.' I use that term for lack of a better word. You ask what there is to do to help move the energy toward the future. It is often a task that needs to be completed before the next step can be taken.

We walk the path one step at a time. We are not shown all the steps at once. But if we diligently apply ourselves and complete each step as it is given, we will progress on the path.

My task was easy. Go ahead and accept the offer for a free half hour of Life Coaching from Eva Liljendahl, who I'd met through an Eva Party in Chicago in April. It's amazing how much clarity you can gain in a focused session with a pro!

As I talked, she would reflect back to me, ask deepening questions, sort it out in issues that turned out to be more than relevant. She asked the key questions that got to the heart of the matter. One such question made it crystal clear, that even if I had all my wishes fulfilled, that if by some magic all that I felt was missing turned up on home turf, Eksjö just didn't cut it. I wasn't here to stay.

She asked a lot of questions about what Sweden represented and what the USA represented. In the course of talking, I got very emotional describing the United States and what it represents to me. Individual freedom and unlimited possibilities. A strong connection with what the Founding Fathers of our country intended. *In God We Trust* in an expansive way, that includes all and respects all life. The American Eagle soaring with vision of a new future. I was homesick for the US. I have no idea why all this emotion is connected to this, but I know I need to trust my heart.

On the face of it, you may wonder why anyone in their right mind would see America as the future, given the current state of affairs. That is one of the advantages of being an intuitive, you can see beyond what is, to what it can be. And somewhere in there, I believe there is a bright future, that this country has the wherewithal to turn things around. I don't think it's an accident that so many people have been involved in human potential. It's got to have an effect and I suspect it's approaching critical mass. All of a sudden the world will have changed in front of your very eyes, for the better. The work is done in the preparation, at least 80 percent is done undercover, when nobody notices.

Fascinating how we interpret things. In hindsight I would say that I connect very strongly with what the United States was intended to be. Whether that means I'm meant to return, I don't know. Time will tell. At least it was not yet. Story of my life. Wait, practice patience, do what is before you.

# Present - Future Exercise

The first time I did the present - future meditation I still lived in Seattle. My therapist gave it to me after a dream where I was crossing a bridge but was too scared to go all the way across. I was shaking with fear so bad I couldn't stand up. I laid down in the middle of the bridge, unable to move on. During my therapy session I found the energy to stand up and cross the bridge. Then I went home and worked the present - future exercise. It helped me step by step to let go of my Seattle life and move to my Sweden life. A big change.

The present - future exercise is a good way to get in touch with our inner dreams and to get direction and help to move toward the future that is calling us. Often what our conscious mind says to do is contrary to what our Higher Self has in mind for us. This exercise puts the Higher Self back in the driver's seat.

There are three elements to keep in mind while doing this exercise. They are
– mindfulness
– gratitude
– compassion
especially for ourselves. Say to yourself 'I open myself to what is necessary and useful in taking these next steps in my process.' Practice watchfulness. How can it happen? Get into a relaxed and meditative state. Imagine yourself in your circle of present life, see it on the floor in front of you, feel all the qualities. Observe who or what is in the circle, notice any

feelings or themes in the present circle. Stay with the present circle until you have a clear sense of the now in your life.

Then, close to the present circle picture another circle - your future circle, which contains the life you are moving into, the parts you want to draw to you. Observe the future circle. How does it feel? Who is present? What are you doing? Sense what was in the present circle that you will leave behind. Some parts will be precise, others more diffuse, some will be nebulous qualities.

YOUR REASONING OR LOGICAL MIND MAY NOT UNDERSTAND, AND THAT'S OK

You can move back and forth between the circles. Notice the difference, what is changing in your life. Then ask if there is any 'homework' for you to do. Whatever you are given is your next step. Spirit rarely gives us the whole plan at once, but if we do the steps given to us, then we will be given the next step. This exercise excites your own life energy and helps you to draw the future to you. Do as much as is comfortable. The temptation may be to do it again without doing the homework - sorry, that isn't going to get you anywhere.

I used this exercise a lot in getting to my house in the country. Some of the early homework was to clean out my closet. My body was very specific - no more high heeled shoes, no more business suits or tight clothes. Until I cleared out the closet, I couldn't move forward. So I packed up several thousand dollars worth of corporate clothing and donated to charity. Then I got instructions how to find my country house. As I would complete one step or homework assignment from the present - future exercise, I would go back in and do the exercise again to get the next step. Part of the process is to trust that your Higher Self is guiding you for your highest good. Your reasoning or logical mind may not understand, and that's OK.

# What about Tenerife?

I went to Tenerife in December of 2001 with some friends. I fell in love with it. The sea, the plants, the food and the possibilities. Nine million visitors per year from all of Europe. For those of you not familiar with this island, a short geography lesson. Tenerife is one of the Canary Islands located off the coast of Africa. It belongs to Spain, and consequently is part of the European Union. Its year around good climate makes it a destination for Europe much like Americans go to Hawaii. The population is very international.

At the time I was in training to be an instructor for Shen Therapy and immediately saw the potential to build a pan European school for this great therapy. If I moved there I could help build up a center that would bring all the different instructors to one place, making it possible to seed the therapy in many more countries than were now 'on-line.'

I got very excited and started to make plans when I came back to Sweden to pull up the stakes. Sometime in the spring I felt the energy shift and go dead. A few months later the Shen organization fell apart. I was scheduled to go pick up my instructor diploma when all this happened and had just started to write my first book. I elected to follow the book writing path...

But what was it about Tenerife that causes people to ask again, if that is not a possibility on the horizon? What was it I loved about it? And do I still want those things?

It doesn't feel like a therapy school is in the wings at this point. But I loved the year around climate. The flowers are beautiful, huge bushes of hibiscus, roses, bougainvillea in various colors, the Spanish influence, the international population, a pretty mountain Teide and sea wherever you look. It has several cities, offering museums, art and a symphony orchestra. In other words big city stuff without having to live in one. An airport that will get you cheaply to any destination in Europe. Relatively cheap to live there. Wonderful nature areas with interesting trees and flowers. A haven for artists. Like all islands, many climate zones in one.

It also turned out I'd had a past life, maybe more, on this island. Looking at the qualities that excited me provides a clue to what I need. It's become very clear to me since, that I want long sandy beaches to walk on, barefoot of course.

I was on Tenerife with several friends and as we flew in from different airports our time there overlapped. I ended up staying with a friend of a friend from the UK for a few days. She suggested I come for three months, then I'd know. I think that is good advice. Wherever I'm tempted to consider, I'll go for three months, hang out, write, paint, meet people, hold a weekly class to see how the energy goes.

My meandering mind then had another thought. I could have a base and keep going to different places for three months at a time, do some teaching with a weekly group, sight see and do all of the above. Wouldn't that be an interesting way to see the world? Check out Hawaii, New Zealand, Australia, the UK, Ireland and maybe China. Or even Japan? Another country I went gaga over. I spent just ten days there visiting my brother as he wrapped up his expat assignment in Nagoya. I don't think I'd like to live there, but I sure would love to go back to see more. And eat the lovely food. My stomach absolutely loved it.

Your process may be about the work you do, or the relationships that form your foundation. Whatever your path, use my ponderings to stimulate your own process. Get yourself deeper into the true path of your life.

# A Healing Center in Hawaii

I'm visiting friends in Colorado and as we sit in group meditation I hear, loud and clear, 'start a healing center in Hawaii.' Hmm... isn't that interesting?

But where on Hawaii? I'd been on Maui and Kauai in the 80's. They did not pop up as prime suspects. But I'd been wanting to go to the big island, the one actually called Hawaii, for a long time. I had another US tour coming up in March, and funny thing, there was a gap in my schedule, that no matter how I worked at it, didn't want to be filled with an Eva Party. So I figured this would be a very good time to go to check out that island on Hawaii.

I did. Met lots of interesting people. Eleven of the thirteen climate zones exist there. Not much in the way of long sandy beaches. Lovely flowers, gardenia, jasmine, plumeria. Heady scents, yes!!! Beautiful and laid back, but not my island. I let it go.

On returning home, I ordered a guide book to Maui. Maybe that's the island they had in mind. I got about half way into it and realized something was missing. Enthusiasm. It didn't feel right. At this time. So I let it go. Figured that whatever was meant to happen would come along at the right time.

Somewhere along the line, an email arrives. From Hawaii. A massage therapist interested in taking courses from me. She's on Oahu, the island with Honolulu and Pearl Harbor. She wonders if I've ever considered Hawaii as a place to live.

She goes on to say she feels my gifts would be much appreciated there. Isn't the way the universe works amazing?

I ponder. Honolulu would have the big city stuff, the nature stuff and the outdoors, an international population, and by the sounds of it ready made pupil(s). But it is expensive. I write back suggesting we set up a class and see how it flies, which would give me a chance to check it out. Sometime this winter. Still waiting for a response. Which is fine. The universe hands out the pieces of the puzzle in its own time. I don't need to know quite yet.

Another beautiful area is Colorado. You can't beat the incredible scenery. I loved the colors! Duh - Color'ado! And very hospitable people. But the climate is a bit rough, with severe weather at the drop of a hat. And no sandy beaches...

Carlsbad, California on the other hand, does have the beach. It's one of those places I've visited many times over the years, hanging out with my friend, meandering through life and lofty discussions. My friend says she always thought I'd end up down there. We'll see. It feels a bit over crowded for my tastes.

While this book has been germinating to fruition, I've made a few more trips to the Hawaiian islands. I discovered Maui is my island. There I felt connected to the land and the people. I loved the community at Unity Church, dancing Five Rhythms at Studio Maui, walking the endless beaches, caressed by the trade winds, kissed by the sun, inspired by Mount Haleakala.

Please use all my ponderings on places as fuel for your own process. You may be thinking of how to redo the garden, or playing with ideas on how to realize your dreams. Whatever your path, let yourself be in the I don't know how, or what, or where - eventually you'll know. It's OK to be in the dark. All the thinking, feeling, what ifs, lists, likes and dislikes are a natural part of crossing the chasm of no data between Z and A.

Love the colors of Color'ado

# It Doesn't Make Sense

I've wondered about the message to start a healing center in Hawaii. I wonder if it wasn't for my friends. She'd gone to a psychic who'd seen the Hawaiian flag in her future. Which was surprising, he said, as normally he would be given at most a country indication, and this was most specifically Hawaii. My healing center message reminded my friend of that prediction. She and her husband would be the perfect hosts for a healing center. I would not. I have books to write, canvases to paint, dancing to teach... and beaches to walk.

Here I am in sunny California. This afternoon we did a walk on the beach. Lovely to have my feet in the water and the sand. The spray of the surf and the sound of the crashing waves are so soothing to my soul. What has been churning through my mind since landing on American soil is 'what am I doing here?' Am I really moving back to this country as my psychic friend has been predicting? Is my homesickness for the country as it is today or for what our Founding Fathers had in mind?

After going to see Sicko this weekend, I wondered why on earth I would want to move back to the USA. It isn't just about the health care, but the whole idea that the leaders of our country are corrupt and greedy. My sense is that the country has slipped off its cogs, that it has lost its reason for being. What the Founding Fathers tried to set up so that it would be a land of the free and brave seems to have been lost. Is it forever? Can the ship be righted again? And more importantly, or should I say personally, do I want to be here to see it go one way or the other?

Which brings me back to the whole question of choice and what do I want? Often, in that space in between, we can't make sense of what is happening. It's hard to get a grip while we are in process. So much is nebulous, unformed, unknown, unspecified. It's not a particularly comfortable space to be in. Like walking in a bog. The ground is not stable.

That's how it feels right now in my life. I'm not sure which end is up. A perfectly appropriate place to be in to be writing this book.

IN THAT SPACE IN BETWEEN, WE CAN'T MAKE SENSE OF WHAT IS HAPPENING

# Head in the Clouds

Lately I've flown on a lot of airplanes. I love sitting in window seats, gazing out at the clouds below. They're like cotton, soft and fluffy and unsolid. They remind me of a fuzzy mind. The unformed. The potential is there, but of what? Looking at the clouds helps my mind wander. Shifting the focus to soft, just letting my thoughts meander, relaxing, spacing out...

Flying has that quality, a gap in time, a blip in space, a moment to let go and just be. Perfect for dreaming and letting the mind go to mush. A perfect moment to not do, to not think, to not be productive.

Spacing in and out in the high skies opens the door to sharper thoughts later on. Like in the middle of the night. The ideas get restless and beckon my attention, wanting to be written down. When I feel restless, I think it's the energy of the ideas that are stocked up. The current demands movement, expression, to be formed into something. Isn't that what creativity is all about? To take the impulse and do something with it?

It starts with clouds like cotton and ends up as what? It's only in exploring and doing something with our creative impulses that we'll find out. At the end of the rainbow could be a pot of gold, but we'll never know if we don't go exploring. So many people tell me they want to write. There is only one way to find out what treasures lie lurking within. You have to start, and then keep going, without attachment to the outcome.

FLYING HAS THAT QUALITY, A GAP IN TIME, A BLIP IN
SPACE, A MOMENT TO LET GO AND JUST BE. PERFECT
FOR DREAMING AND LETTING THE MIND GO TO MUSH.

# Do the Experience and Trust the Universe

Often, it's the path that leads to the goal that is key. The outcome is truly secondary. It may not be at all what you expected. In writing a book, it is the very process of piecing it together that is the journey. Sure it's wonderful to hold the finished book in my hands, but the bulk of the experience is in the doing. The sparks that fly as ideas uncork, the excitement of ahas as the fingers dance on the keyboard, that is the bulk of the outcome. As we create, we are the outcome. We become the product in doing the experience.

Many people report a sense of emptiness after completing a project or major milestone. Even a sense of disappointment. They had so looked forward to reaching the goal. But when they got there, the anticipated emotion isn't there. Partially the answer lies in the living of the expectation, that before we even got there, we've already experienced many of the emotions. While we are on our way, we are having a lot of experiences, that actually are the outcome, more so than the finished product.

Does this make you uncomfortable? The very idea of just doing it for the sake of doing it, without knowing where the path may take you? I perceive that to be a common stumbling block. Inside, you sense that you may end up on a road you hadn't planned on. You may be presented with growth opportunities that feel, quite frankly, very scary. Most of us are not comfortable with success.

The status quo is often more comfortable than embarking on a new treasure hunt. Who knows what you will find? Do you think JK Rowling had any idea her Harry Potter would be so successful? No. But she wrote it anyway. The story was there for her to write and she followed through on that impulse. She did the experience and trusted the universe.

Look at all the explorers who went sailing off to find the new world, at a time when consensus had us believe the earth was flat. They really didn't know if there was an end of the world, that would rather abruptly have plunged them into nothingness. They went anyway. They did the experience and trusted the universe, perhaps with a bit of prayer to help them along.

DO THE EXPERIENCE AND TRUST THE UNIVERSE

# Choices

Although we incarnate on earth to learn certain lessons, burn karmic ribbons, honor agreements and experience life as human beings, we do have choice. Which means that even the best laid plans go awry. Just think of your last trip - did everything go as you had imagined? Probably not, stuff happened along the way. What is an agreement? It is a promise, that when entered into, was right - in that moment. As time passes, it may not suit us anymore. There may be other choices, that we feel are more appropriate.

This is kind of a round-about way to lead into my thoughts on my process and choice. Up to now, every time I have moved or made a major change, there has been a compelling thread to guide me there. It has been for the sake of a job, a project, a completion, a karmic ribbon, an agreement... but this time, there is a different feel. Although I see disciples in my future, they can be in several places. It doesn't feel like there is only one option available. This time it is about choice.

One friend remarked how fortunate I am, to be able to go just about anywhere in the world. But unlimited choice is not an easy life lesson. There are so many variables, and so many possibilities, how does one choose?

As I had the lead on disciples, I decided to test that thread, to see where I might have interested students. Then it's up to me to decide if I want to live there. I am responsible for the choices I make. And the only way to know if a choice is right, or rather, to see where a choice will take you, is to step into the unknown and cross that chasm of no data. Scary, yes! It's no wonder it makes me a bit nervous. There is a vulnerability in stepping into a new something. Exciting, and yet uncomfortable. You both want it and not. From past experience, I know the discomfort will pass, but nonetheless it is there.

So what choices do I have? I can go anywhere in the USA and Europe. As a writer I may even be able to go hang out in New Zealand or Australia. I would prefer to be in an English speaking country with a mild climate and close to the beach. But you never know what is around the corner... what life choices are down your path. Each step you take, can alter the forks down the road. As one door closes, another one opens.

YOU NEVER KNOW WHAT IS AROUND THE CORNER...
WHAT LIFE CHOICES ARE DOWN YOUR PATH

# Working with Resistance

At a recent Eva Party, I was asked 'how do you work with resistance?' Good question. As a matter of fact, a VERY good question. And equally important, how do you tell the difference between resistance and 'not the right path'?

Let's start with looking at how to tell if something is yours to do. The ancient Hawaiian Hunas believed in following the path with the highest life energy. You can too. In a meditative state, you can get a feel for the energy, or the light potential of different paths. A poor choice is anything that intentionally harms another human being, is ethically wrong or interferes with the life choices of another person.

What does resistance feel like? Hmm, imagine a five year old digging in her heels, arms firmly anchored across her chest, shaking her head, saying 'no way' and you have a pretty good idea of the feeling state involved. Resistance is your ego, your personality self, your ungrown up self wanting to stay put. It is like a mental fence that rejects out of hand any new idea. As souls in human bodies, we are here to grow. So whatever you resist persists. Eventually we get to have all the experiences possible on the earth plane. So why wait until next life? Why not take the plunge now and meet your resistance?

Say hello to it. Approach it with whatever emotion you have about it. Talk to it. Scream at it if you are so inclined. But don't ignore it, because it is not going to go away. Then plunge into it with gusto, or dip your toe in. It doesn't matter if you go whole hog or nibble, but DO IT!

The book before this one came about because I finally realized I couldn't ignore it any longer. I did not want to write a book in Swedish, no way, it was not in my plans at all. I wanted to write this book, on the space in between. But to get here, I had to surrender into the resistance and write *The Courage to Live*. Once I did, a whole new path opened up for me.

WHILE IN RESISTANCE, WE ACTUALLY SHUT OFF THE
NATURAL LIFE ENERGY

So how did I surrender? Not gracefully, that's for sure. Friends kept pestering me to write, and one full moon weekend I let loose, in an 'I'll show you' mode. I wrote down lots of notes and ideas, fired off comments, put it all in a file, and forgot about it.

I went on tour, and a few months later my writing was stuck. Imagine my surprise when I opened the file and discovered an entire outline for a book. By then, I realized it was mine to do. I had a lot of emotion to work through, so the first draft was quite different than the final book. But it freed me up. I had to write it in order to be able to move on. If I hadn't written it, I wouldn't be doing this book. I'd still be stuck in resistance. Petulance, is another way to put it. In no way does resistance feel pleasant. Ornery, obstinate, you get the picture.

While in resistance, we actually shut off the natural life energy. Once we let it loose, it can flow smoothly again. Emotions are energy in motion. So is creativity. If we block it, we get tired and feel unwell. It is of equal importance to express ourselves creatively as it is to experience our emotions. Moving the life energy involves moving the physical body and nourishing it as well. If you learn to listen to your body, and indulge your impulses, without getting too mental about it, you'll do fine.

Working through resistance has a lot to do with a change in perspective. It's an opening of the senses to let yourself try something different. To simply focus on this is before me, I do it. It's OK to charge full steam ahead, all the while feeling squirmy and wishing you were somewhere else.

Instead of running away from resistance, stick with it, like glue. Sit there until you've sausaged your way through it. The sausage expression comes from a friend of mine. She knew I'd had a hard time writing some stuff. I didn't know what to say, or where to start and I felt very nervous. I had to force myself to sit at my computer until I got it done, feeling very squirmy the whole time. I wanted to escape, but I didn't.

My friend had something she'd put off for ages. But she told herself, 'now Kristina, you are going to stay here until you have sausaged your way through this, just like Eva does.' She got it done, and in the process experienced a tremendous relief.

You can too.

# Take Nothing for Granted

I find it amusing, in a way, that my own life is in an in between state. Which makes it easy for me to mirror the emotional state of not knowing which end is up. Where am I going and why? What do I want? What is important to me now? These are all questions that naturally surface in between.

It makes some people uneasy when you talk of change.

- I thought you decided you were a writer? they'll ask.
- You need to find your niche and stay there.
- Settle down and find your roots.

I could go on.

Change is unsettling, because it questions all that is taken for granted. All the built in assumptions on how our world looks is suddenly up for debate and question. Yes it is unsettling. Even to me.

I've been told my middle name is change. I can own that. But not change for the sake of change. Change for the sake of growth. Change for the sake of discovering something new. Isn't that what creativity and invention is all about? To find another way to view things, to discover new solutions, new ways of healing, new ways to express our humanity?

So change is not a bad thing, but it does push our limits, asks us to take a step into some unknown. No matter how many times you've done it, you still feel the butterflies in your stomach. The trick is to let them be butterflies. Be friends with the stirring in your gut. It's a good sign that you may be on to something.

Ideas are surfacing, like a recheck of sorts. Just because I've been going down one path for some time now, doesn't mean I'll want to keep doing that. Going out and doing talks to promote my books was fun, for a while. I notice it doesn't have the same charge or excitement anymore. Partly it's because I've become comfortable with standing up and ad libbing in front of a group. Although on my last tour, to bookstores in the USA, I did get nervous. I discovered that it's much harder to get the energy flowing to an audience where the people are not connected to each other. Actually, I've observed this earlier, but I was reminded how much more fun it is to work a group that's already started to form a Master Mind. I hear your questions already, please explain... what is a Master Mind? Be patient, it's in the next chapter.

For the last few days, I have been busy mentally, thinking about what is important now. Reflecting on how my needs have changed. When I moved to Sweden I needed to go deep within. I did not have much energy for outward social interaction. Today I am much more extroverted, in fact I need more interaction.

When I moved here, the job market was closed for someone like me, with foreign education and foreign experience. Today that is apparently not so. The thought surfaced, would I want to get a 'real' job now? For so long, that was my most dear wish. In the end I realized it wasn't going to happen. Now that it might be a possibility, do I want it? Or is it just the lure of a steady paycheck and a structured life? Would it feed my soul? It depends on what it is of course. It doesn't feel like it would be my first choice, but my point is, allow yourself to examine every question that comes up.

Take nothing for granted. As you evolve, your needs change, your way of interacting with the world changes, even your interests change. Once we've done an experience enough times, we don't need to repeat it.

Dream a dream, manifest it, experience it. Then it's time to dream another dream. So let's take nothing for granted. This is so key in any change or transition work. It doesn't matter if it's a simple personal decision or the design of a new world government. To get to the new, you can not take anything for granted. You have to let go of your basic beliefs about what is true.

DREAM A DREAM, MANIFEST IT, EXPERIENCE IT. THEN IT'S TIME TO DREAM ANOTHER DREAM.

# Master Mind

In the last chapter, I mentioned the concept of a Master Mind. One of the early pioneers in the human potential movement, Napoleon Hill, wrote several books on the hidden secrets to success. The following is an excerpt from Wikipedia on Napoleon Hill and the concept of the Master Mind:

Hill is also credited with coining the phrase 'Master Mind'. The 'Master Mind' may be defined as: 'coordination of knowledge and effort in a spirit of harmony, between two or more people, for the attainment of a definite purpose.' In Think and Grow Rich, Hill discusses his creation of Master Mind groups and how these groups could multiply an individual's brain power and continually motivate positive emotions. However, the Master Mind was a deeper and more powerful connection than mere synergetic cooperation would suggest, and requires an understanding of Hill's belief's about the brain and the nature of energy (particularly thought energy) within Thomas Edison's cosmological understanding of matter and energy. In describing the Philosophy of Achievement, Hill was careful in his writings to examine the brain as a sending/receiving station for thought; and for the first time in history explained to the world that like-mindedness had a physical basis. Hence the Master Mind, governed by the laws of mutual attraction, could only exist if like-mindedness was achieved between individuals. Scientists had only recently (in Hill's time) shown that the brain was the true source of thought, and hence like-mindedness could now have a true physical underpinning from the point of view of science.

Hill states there are two characteristics of the Master Mind principle; one is economic, the other psychic. Economic advantages arise from sharing and cooperation with others utilizing the Philosophy of Achievement. As to the other, Hill states: 'No two minds ever come together without, thereby, creating a third, invisible, intangible force which may be likened to a third mind.' This force, Hill reasoned, was tremendously valuable and ultimately the source of true wealth. Hill also believed that the human mind is a form of energy, part of it spiritual in nature. He states that when the minds of two people are coordinated in a spirit of harmony, the spiritual units of energy of each mind form an affinity, which constitutes the 'psychic' phase of the Master Mind.

I love how the Internet has become one large information booth! Anytime you set up a network or peer learning group, you have the potential to create a Master Mind. We are far more connected than most people realize.

In our *Creative Dance* group, we'd had a teacher, then she moved away. We decided to continue on our own, to collectively take over her role. In the beginning we'd decide on a theme for the next get together. We soon saw that we were so intuitively synched that we could let go of setting a theme. The Master Mind was at work. All we had to do before our weekly sessions was tune in to the group and bring music and exercises that came to mind. It was fun to experience the synchronicity.

In the Michael group the channels will do group chats on the Internet with participants from all over the globe. When all of us focus our energies in meditations and exercises, you can almost touch the connecting threads. Imagine what social media can do as we tune in and network with each other. Maybe just the forerunner to something else?

# Expand Your Thinking

How do you do expand your thinking? It is not an intellectual or logical exercise at all, although the end result seems to be of the mind, a thought. Bear with me as I meander a bit.

I am fascinated with and by groups. It is simply more effective to move the energy in a group than one by one. OK, it could just be a personal bent of mine. I've been reflecting that it is not feeding my soul to travel all over and meet with each group just once. I long to work with a group over an extended period of time. What if, I get to work with a group with a purpose? Where there is a common interest among the individuals? Where each and every one is heading in a similar direction?

I would use all my tools from the creative and therapeutic arena. We would practice them together and on each other, to end up at a place where we had expanded our thinking. The trick in presenting a course like that is to get people beyond the mental idea, that it actually is about thinking. I have that challenge with my writing courses. People come expecting to be totally mental. Writing comes from stirring the life energy, moving the body, being present in emotions, playing with painting, letting go - not from thinking until your head hurts.

To expand your thinking, you have to go beyond the mind. To expand your thinking, you have to involve the body. To expand your thinking you have to engage the emotions, pesky little things! To expand your thinking, you have to connect with your Soul.

YOU HAVE TO GO BEYOND THE MIND

# Every Place is Good for Something

My first encounter with Astrocartography was years ago in Seattle. It was fairly early in the understanding of what all the planetary lines meant. The astrologer who looked at my map, interpreted any place with lots of intersecting lines to be a good one. Even then, I wondered if that was right.

About seven years ago, I took another foray into the science of relocation astrology. With the map I ordered came Jim Lewis' book on what the lines actually meant. I read and looked and read and pondered. The only conclusion I went away with was 'every place is good for something.' I've included the map on the next page spread.

While in the San Francisco Bay area of late, I had lunch with Emily Baumbach, an astrologer and Michael channel. Naturally, she was curious about my potential moving plans. Turns out she works a bit with astrocartography. A timely reminder of a perhaps useful tool for my pending move.

With the Internet at my fingertips, I found some very interesting new material. An American astrologer, Robert Couteau, had studied the charts of quite a few famous people as well as events and nations from an Astrocartography perspective. I was intrigued to read that the Least Aspected Planet, or Transcendental Planet, was key.

Ah, I thought. At long last, someone who has made sense of this Astrocartography business and what it really means. My Least Aspected Planets, also known as Transcendental Planets, are:

1 - Mercury, Primary Transcendental

2 - Jupiter and Uranus, Secondary Transcendental

On an astrocartography map, you see not just one line for each planet, but four: the Ascendant, the Descendant, the IC or Imum Coeli and the MC or Medium Coeli, in plain English the Mid heaven.

For many years, I lived on the west coast of the United States, where my Pluto IC line lies. The Mercury IC line intersects the Azores Islands. I went there to what I thought would be a two week vacation. I ended up writing a big chunk of the book *Secrets of Transformation* while there. Does it mean I need to live there? No, but it shows that Mercury did indeed have a strong influence there, as indicated by geographical astrology. So this guy is on to something with the placement of Transcendental planets.

Mercury represents the mind and intellect. It is an airy planet, associated with all forms of communication and the in-flow and out-flow of intelligence and communication.

I also have a Mercury line that goes through northern India. I was one of fifteen Swedish artists selected for a TellusArt project in India, doing exhibitions and workshops with leading artists from Asia and Scandinavia. Right on that Mercury line. I felt seen and heard in a much broader sense. It's like people understood what my art was about.

Moving on to my secondaries, which are of equal weight, astrologically speaking, we have Jupiter and Uranus. Uranus is known as the planet of freedom and revolutionary vision, the urge for change, and the ability to visualize new possibilities. Jupiter represents the principle of expansion and is the planet of faith, positivism, hope, and morality

Let's look at where Jupiter and Uranus show up on my world map. Jupiter passes through Greenland (brrr...) and eastern South America. Tango anyone, in Argentina? Another Jupiter line passes through central Australia, up through Bali and the south of Japan. I loved Japan, to visit anyway. The food made my body very happy. The curvy Jupiter line passes through northern Russia (more brrr…) down through the Middle East and east Africa. I'm fascinated with east Africa, in a historic sense. Loved *Out of Africa*, the *Flame Trees of Thika*, reading about the adventure of Beryl Markham.

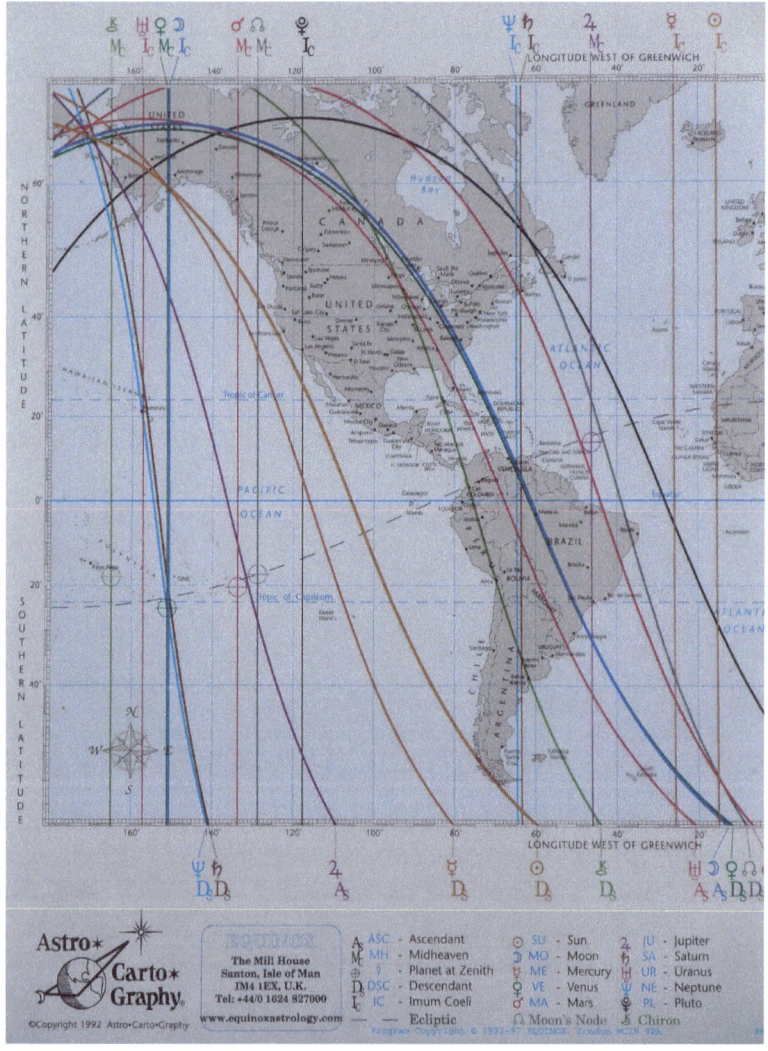

Last year I finally got to visit Australia. While we're on the train from Perth to Sydney, I have one of those big aha moments. I tune into a new wish for abundance. To be really well off so that I can travel in style and not worry about the money. Later I realized that insight happened right as we're crossing that Jupiter line.

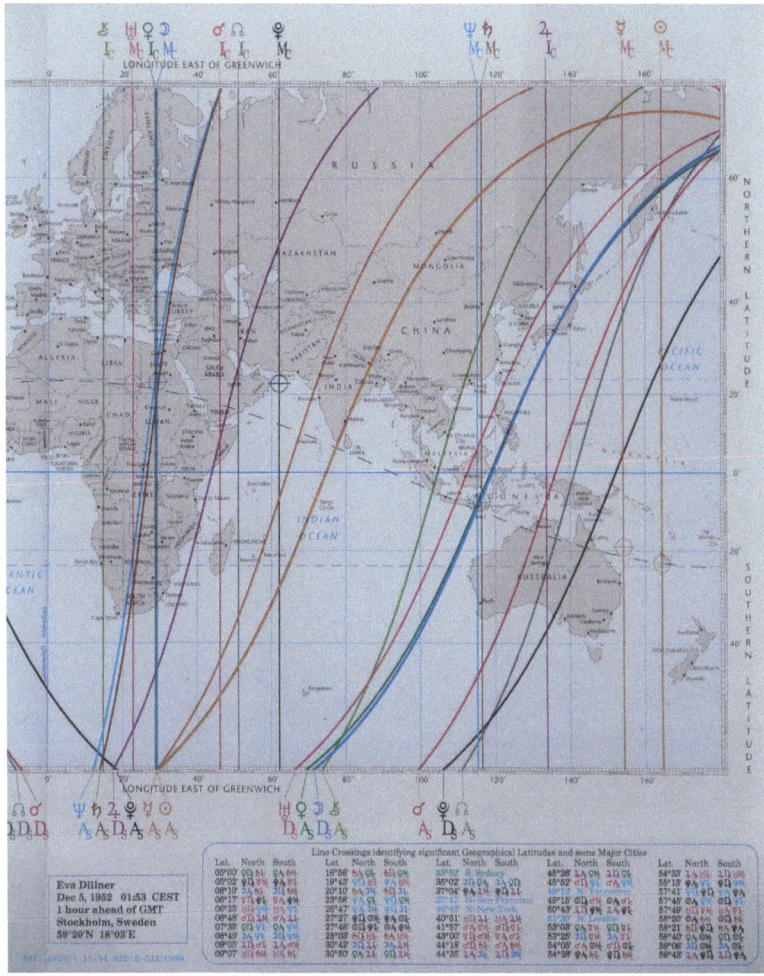

Uranus we find in Hawaii, and up through the middle of Africa, eastern Europe and the west of Finland. I have a disproportionate number of friends who were born in Finland. A coincidence? I don't think so. The curvy Uranus line passes west of Japan, down via Indonesia, through the middle of south America to slice through Florida, and up via Illinois to Canada and Alaska (even more brrr...).

A planet that isn't included in Robert Couteau's work, but does appear on my Equinox map, is Chiron, named for the Greek god, the wounded healer. I mention it here, since at the moment I live right on my Chiron IC line. Not so strange that my time here has been focused on healing.

Looking beyond the Transcendental Planets, I have a Sun line right through the Canary Islands, another place that really appealed to me, that felt like home. Under the sun line you become more you.

# Savasana - The Death Pose in Yoga

I've taken many yoga classes, but it wasn't until I arrived in Sweden that I found the program that has stuck with me. I think one of the reasons I like it so much is the savasana. When we were learning, we would do an active yoga pose, then the savasana. Then another active pose, followed by the savasana. Boy did this suit my way of doing things!

So what then, is the savasana?

It is called the death pose. You lie flat on your back with arms diagonally at your sides, palms facing up. The legs are also relaxed in a V formation. You enter a space between awake and asleep, that void space I keep talking about. At least the objective is to be in the void. Like all human endeavors, we practice so that once in a while we may actually achieve that space.

We can take the idea of doing and resting into everything we do. Inserting pauses in between exercise routines feels more natural to me. Inserting pauses into our daily lives is essential for our well being. A short, or long, pause can make all the difference in the world.

When hiking in the woods, stopping for a rest and a feed feels good. We get a chance to catch up with ourselves. Be still and observe what is around us. Take in the smells and sounds and sights. Perhaps not the exact intention of a serious yoga devotee, but you get the idea. Quit rushing through life, pause and catch your breath in between.

Make friends with voids.

# Swedish Hibernation - Where Creative Genius is Born

You may not know it, but Sweden is quite a unique country. A little Viking nation with 9 million here and half a million abroad. A country the size of California with the population of Belgium.

When I was about to return here in the nineties, I seriously thought I was going back to the corporate world. So I did a lot of research on companies. Sweden is truly an export nation. We have a disproportionate number of international corporations like IKEA, Ericsson, Volvo and SKF to name a few. And who hasn't heard of Pippi Longstocking and her creator Astrid Lindgren? Or the best selling author Stieg Larsson and his heroine Lisbeth Salander? There are three major export countries of music in the world. Number one is the United States and number two is the United Kingdom, quite like you would expect. But who is number three? Yep, little Sweden. You have heard of Abba, I presume?

We are also very good at inventions. An impressive array of clever products have come out of this little country. Inventions like the zipper and dynamite are all Swedish in origin, and they are just the tip of the iceberg. The ball bearing, Celsius thermometer, Skype, GPS, the safety match, the adjustable spanner, Tetra Pak, Losec medicine, the computer mouse, Linné's classification system for plants, animals and minerals, the separator and milking machine, the propeller, the turbo engine for cars, Styrofoam, the pacemaker, the AXE telephone exchange, the three point safety belt, the steam turbine. The list is long.

DAYDREAMING IS A LOST ART

What makes us so creative and productive? I have a theory about that. Traditionally, in order to survive in this climate, you had to be resourceful. The long dark winters far away from your neighbors is fertile ground for the imagination. Add to that the encouragement to explore science and the arts. It's like there is enough space in the ethers to think clearly.

I have this idea we should offer reverse charter. In winter. Hibernation vacations. Incubate, dream and just be in the dark. Spread the visitors out to little cottages and work with them on going within type creative processes. Show them how to be in the stillness of snow, to listen for the quiet as the snow flakes drift down in the darkness. Let them experience the exhilaration of the winter colors here.

We could offer incubation for creativity. I even have the marketing slogan:

### SWEDISH HIBERNATION
#### WHERE CREATIVE GENIUS IS BORN

Innovation comes naturally with long dark winters and deep woods. The uncrowded silence in our woods and by our lakes is unique. It's what attracts the Germans, Dutch and English to come visit in droves during summer.

- What will they do in winter?

That is the whole point, it is not about doing, but about being. Sitting in front of the fire, walking in the woods, being quiet, sleeping a lot. I find that I sleep more in winter, I just can't get up while it's still dark. One of my friends says 'the Sun and I have an agreement, he gets up first' and she lives in California!

Daydreaming is a lost art. Staring into space. Doing nothing, just letting our thoughts go in neutral. Going beyond boredom. Watching the rain and snow fall. Listening to the quiet sounds of winter.

The whole experience is about the smallness. All together in a given region there are cabins and family run pensions and B&B's that together could do an entire charter flight. And it's in the personal and small encounter that you get to experience the uniqueness of a Swedish winter. We could bill them as creative incubation retreats. Rest and recuperation from the madness of life in the big city.

Ideas, those I have plenty of...

# Indigestion

After an eventful summer, with many meetings and much to sort, it is no wonder I'm having a hard time digesting it all. My mind can't seem to get a wrap on what is going on. I am having a hard time just landing and settling down. Like I'm still going, even though I am stopped.

This afternoon I cleaned house, and that helped to clear up the energies. I felt a need to paint, to do something non verbal, to just let the energies flow. They sure did. Confusion is such a great creative state. When you don't know what you are doing, when you can't even see what you are putting on the canvas because the tears are dimming your sight, some really great stuff can happen.

I felt relief only to experience indigestion. So much to process. We think it is the food we ate, but instead it's the emotions and thoughts we are trying to process. It gets too much and the stomach says 'hello, no more of this!'

There is some great fear lurking here. Of what I am not sure. It feels better when I tell myself I can take it slow, one step at a time, that I don't have to take the leap in one fell swoop. Whatever that leap is about. For sure there is emotion in here. Great creative potential perhaps. I have not been writing or painting regularly so it may just be a pent up creative energy wanting out. I do have rather a lot to say.

I'm used to letting it all hang out with my fears and inadequacies. But not with my greatness. Could it be that I am afraid of success, of really being in the spotlight? Is the fear that I'm just ordinary or that I am not? Discomfort and indigestion are making themselves known.

THERE IS EMOTION IN HERE
GREAT CREATIVE POTENTIAL PERHAPS

# Confusion as Healer

Confusion is sometimes a good thing. In the early nineties I trained to be a Certified Hypnotherapist. One of the induction techniques we learned, in addition to all the regular relaxation and deepening approaches, was confusion. The goal in hypnosis is to get past the mental fences that we all have. To get that iron mind to relax long enough to let the soul peek through. Our teacher likened it to the sun being hidden behind clouds.

Confusion instructions are rapid fire, conflicting with each other. One way is to give map quest type instructions, but keep changing them: no that's not right, go left, then right... and so on. It is a rare mind that can hold on to control. When it lets go, the client relaxes and you can get down to the real business.

Many hold an idea that confusion is bad. I say just the opposite. Confusion is a great state to get you into creative and healing spaces. Often in confusion there are conflicting emotions. They are just bursting at the seams to get out, all you have to do is help them along.

That gap in space, from rigid holding on, to surrendering into flow, is what this whole book is about. When the client surrenders to the confusion in hypnotherapy, or any other healing modality for that matter, all the emotions come bubbling out, all at once, like greased lightning. And that is perfectly as it should be. Once the catharsis subsides, clarity can be found. It's been there all along, underneath.

But what do most people suggest when you are all wound up and confused?

- Take it easy, they say.

- You need to land and be still, they will comment.

- If you just calm down, all things will come to you when they are ready, is another favorite.

All these people mean well, but they don't understand following the life energy. Many people think that to be creative you have to be calm and collected. Many creative people show symptoms of being manic depressive, or bi-polar. Are they?

I don't think so. They are just creative. The greatest healing breakthroughs I've seen are when a client, or myself, have been at our wits end. When nervous breakdown might have been the diagnosis of the traditional view. I think it is great news, finally the cork is out and all that has been held in has a chance to get out and be healed. Afterward there is a calm.

Who said being the same every day is normal? What if normal is more like the weather? One day it is stormy, another rainy, another still not a breeze is stirring and once in a while the sun shines. What if we looked at emotional weather the same way?

I see that when we give in to that flow of life energy, magic does happen. Instead of fretting that I can't sleep, I get up and write or paint or tone or dance, or whatever I feel the need to do. All I am doing is responding to the natural life energy.

I think confusion is just pent up a lot of stuff at one time. Trying to calm down just puts the lid on, and then where are you? Stuck. My opinion, not necessarily the truth with a capital T.

# Fear of Failure

One of the unsettling things about being in a between space is the not knowing which way is up. Wondering what the heck you are doing. Wondering why you feel compelled to do certain things. Not being able to answer what your plans are, long term. At best, you know some priorities, or, at this moment I need to do this.

As I laid awake I marveled at how unsettled my intestines were feeling. Why was the sacral region all stirred up? Was it anticipation? Worry? Fear of failure? Aah... there we have it. In my head I was reviewing my path forward. Next week I go help move my parents into assisted living. Then there is the book fair. In my head I was reviewing and planning how I would do these tasks and realized I felt nervous.

Moving my parents is no small task. They will be moving into a much smaller space, so once we have moved the essentials they now need, I get to somehow sort through all the rest. They are not like me, who more than once has left it all behind to start over. No, my parents lived almost 40 years in a big home, and it feels like they haven't thrown anything away for the past 50. You can accumulate a lot of stuff in 50 years. They have moved several times since leaving their big home, but the amount of stuff has not dwindled appreciably, so in a way it is almost harder to get a grip on what they have.

In every persons life there comes that time where you have to let go of the material things. At this stage in their life, they will need their 'huggy blankets' in addition to the basics. It falls on me to sort out what is what. And that makes me nervous. How do I sort what is important to them? How do I do this so it is a somewhat smooth transition? They have so much stuff, the task feels overwhelming.

Actually, it isn't so much a fear of failure I am experiencing, but a sense of overwhelment. I'm not sure I'll be able to get it all done without loosing it.

As I write, I realize the theme is sorting out what is essential. That is where I am in my own process. What is essential for me? I often get asked how financially successful my book tours are. To most people, the measure of success would be that I sold a lot of books, or that I had huge crowds at my talks and classes.

TO HELP YOU SEE A DIFFERENT SLANT

As I talk about my travels, I realize I measure by a different drummer. I talk of the connections, social and otherwise, what I got to see and experience, as well as the talks, classes and book signings. To me the travel is key. I could probably be doing something else that would take me around the world. Selling just isn't my thing, but unfortunately it is part of the earth plane game.

So if I go around the world and have wonderful experiences but I don't sell enough books to break even, does that make me a failure? How do I measure what I do? What is important to me and what is important to others?

I am often in the position of being questioned, in my motives, in my modus operandi, until I realize I need to get comfortable with my way of doing it. When I understand and accept that I have a different guide post, another angle to view it from, I then share it with others. It is my job to help you see a different slant.

# Divine Synchronicity

All is in Divine order, is one of my favorite sayings. Inspired by the writings of Florence Scovel Shinn and Emmett Fox, two people who wrote wonderful and inspiring books on how the Divine Design operates in our lives. I even named my company and web site Divine Design. At first it felt big, pretentious, to call my little business Divine Design, but as I meditated on it, it made all the sense in the world.

Divine Design is simply natural law, or the solution for the highest good for all. Divine Design comes about if we don't interfere with the energy of the universe. But we humans have a propensity to poke our nose into everything instead of trusting the God force to help us along. I think that is one of the biggest challenges we face, to learn to trust the natural flow of life.

Along with feeling overwhelmed with all the details coming at me, I also see that there is a Divine synchronicity in all that is happening. I had sent in the application for assisted living for my parents before taking off on a two month tour. As the Swedish way is to stand in line for a long time - there is always a bureaucratic wait - I figured it would take many months before we'd hear anything. Imagine my surprise, when one week after coming home, there is an offer for an apartment in the number one choice on our list. We have a week to check it out and decide.

Now isn't it amazing that the offer comes now? When I am home and not on the road? What is even more amazing is that

I have time to deal with it. I had purposely scheduled myself home in plenty of time before the Gothenburg Book Fair, so that I not only would get over my jet lag, but also have enough space and time to pull myself together. The first week I was home, I took care of all the remaining details, like printing out press releases, making posters, check lists, packing bookmarks and all the rest. At the time I wondered a bit, thinking I have plenty of time, but there was this energy pushing me to do it. So when the call came about the assisted living, I was free to deal with it.

That is Divine timing. The universe couldn't have picked a better time for this to happen. It's funny, the last time they moved, my brother just 'happened' to be on a business trip in Sweden, and was able to spend three days with them during that move. The universe makes available the right resources at the right time.

# Turbo Times

As I go through the process of moving my parents into assisted living, there are lots of things to deal with. Like purchasing bedding, linens, underwear, nightclothes, lamps - you name it. Then there are all the decisions, what to bring and what to leave. Trying to make the new environment as homey and familiar as possible, as quickly as possible. It's a lot. I try to tackle the highest, most essential priority and let go of the rest. But with so many things to deal with in a short time, it's not surprising I lie awake at night, planning, churning, twisting and turning. There is simply too much to deal with.

What makes all this even more challenging is the fact that I am alone in dealing with it. My parents have moved three times in the last three years, never really unpacking in each place. Their house was over 3000 square feet, and even though they moved into places about half the size, they still kept all the rugs, paintings, teddy bears, knickknacks, pillows - you name it! Add to that the change in countries and voltages, and their absolute inability to throw anything away. All the pictures they have taken are still in the envelopes, and although there are picture albums, they are empty. Somehow they never got around to it.

So now, here I am, trying to deal with all this stuff that has taken a lifetime to accumulate. With mom's dementia, everything is helter-skelter in closets and boxes. With a confused brain, there can be no organization. I suspect all the excess

STUFF makes it even harder to cope. I feel totally over-whelmed trying to sort through it.

### TURBO TIMES

Even though I now see how I can do a rough sort, pile all the rugs here, all the paintings there, all the clothes in a closet - there is so much of everything it boggles the mind. I want to go home and throw every excess item out in my own place, and I do not have much to begin with! I'm making teddy bear piles, blanket piles, towel piles. It amazes me how much stuff there is. The silverware can just as easily be found in the dresser as in a box, or even in the kitchen. Dirty sheets are crammed in on a shelf with lamp shades. It's unbelievable. And all the time dad keeps calling wondering when I'm coming to visit.

I feel overwhelmed.

I have a really hard time relaxing and letting this process take whatever time it takes. I'd like to get it done and over with. Heave out whatever they are no longer in need of, sell off and close out the project and get on with my life. Impatience.

Breathe deeply, relax and let go. Easier said than done in turbo times.

# The Courage to Fail

Sitting here watching the movie *Shadows in the Sun*, about a writer who had one fantastic novel and then nada. He hadn't written in twenty years, not since his wife died. Long and the short of it, he was afraid.

Afraid that he couldn't do it anymore. Afraid that whatever he would write, it could never be as good as his first novel. Afraid that nothing could eclipse it. Afraid that he had lost it. Afraid to face his pain. Yes, all of that. But most of all, afraid to fail. Afraid to be human.

Why is failure such a big thing? Why do we think it is not OK to fail? Why is it such a big deal to make a mistake? Isn't that what life is? One big laboratory, where we get to try things, sometimes we succeed, sometimes we fail.

You know it's funny. Big failures often precede big successes. If you look at the people who make fortunes, you'll often find that they have one or more bankruptcies behind them. What if failing is a precursor to success?

Think of it this way. When we fail, we're really finding out what doesn't work. That way we can adjust our plan, try something different, and maybe get it right the next time. Or at least get a little closer.

So the next time you flub up, pat yourself on the back. Yes, now I know one more way to not do it. See, you learn from doing. The only way to find the path is to check out where the roads go. You have to step into it to know. Sometimes it's a pile of manure, other times you hit the jackpot. So applaud your less than perfect efforts.

## LIFE IS ONE BIG LABORATORY

Let yourself be human.

Make a big splash!

Give yourself permission to test, to try, to see what happens if I do it this way? Be adventerous in the little things. Paint outside the lines. Break rules of how things should be done. It's OK to be different. Where do you think new ideas come from?

# Going Full Circle?

This fall has been hard work. Moving my parents and doing the Gothenburg Book Fair as well as the Alternative Network Fair in Oslo calls for some time out. I started looking for some place to go loll around a long sandy beach, and ended up booking a trip to Tenerife, in Puerto de la Cruz. It was the place I was all ready to move to in the spring of 2002, to start an international Shen Therapy school, when the universe put the brakes on. The energy just wasn't there anymore, but I couldn't understand why. A few months later the Shen organization went through a major split and I was cast adrift and started writing.

Here I am, five books and six years later. I started picking up the Shen thread when I wrote extensively about it in my last Swedish book, introducing the concept of perpetual learning groups and creating meditation exercises to learn the energy flows. My focus has shifted from training therapists to giving people the skills to help themselves in self help groups. Since the book *Courage to Live* came out, I've been asked about courses in Shen, as well as the other creative and therapeutic processes I describe in the book.

It just so happens that one of my talks in Oslo will be on Shen. It wasn't until I'd booked my trip to Tenerife that I started putting the pieces together. I seem to be coming full circle. Picking up the Shen thread and traveling to that place I fell in love with. It may be a completion to let go and move on, or a picking up where I left off. The path is seldom straight on, and the universe doesn't explain how it all is going to fit in the end.

WE NEED TO LEARN TO TRUST THE UNIVERSE

I can tell I haven't been writing for some time. My life has been far too full of practical details lately, and not enough creative dream time.

It only took me a few days to feel into and reminisce about Tenerife, to realize there is no energy for me to go there at this time. I needed to book the trip to start the connection to memory lane. Once I got far enough down that memory lane, the realization dropped in to cancel the trip. Which I did this morning. Why?

There is something delicious about changing one's mind. To allow that savoring of what if? Is this what I want? How do I feel about it? Some paths you have to go quite a ways down, or up, to realize this is not my path, now. Then have the courage to admit to yourself that it doesn't feel right. You don't have to understand why, or be able to explain why you abruptly changed your mind. It's your life and you get to live it your way.

See, I don't think you can figure it all out ahead of time. You won't actually know how you will feel, until you have the ticket booked, or the keys in your hand, or actually live in the situation you think you want.

About a month later I understand what it was all about. An emergency necessitates the move of my mother to a dementia facility. At the exact time I would have gone to Tenerife. We can never know why we get such strong signals to change our plans. We need to learn to trust the universe.

# The Reluctant Shaman

I ran across some notes from an exercise we did in the Life Mission group I helped run in Seattle in the mid 1990's. In this exercise, we worked with each other to answer the question intuitively of what the person does. Those of us in the group knew each other fairly well and were all a ways along the path, so tuning in and trusting the answers wasn't new to us. The person being 'read' sits in front of the group, with her back to the group, so everyone is facing the same way, ahead. Everyone gets into a quiet meditative state and the question is asked 'what does Eva do?' (or Dick or Merrill-Jan or whoever is the front person). As answers come sifting into awareness, they are spoken out loud, without censoring or stopping to make logical sense out of it. Just let it flow.

I thought it would be useful to include the answers they got for me here.

**What does Eva do?**

- Gathers elements together puts them in a new form
- Firestarter
- Synthesizer
- Recreating
- Tools - reshaping
- Transformation
- Transition change
- Bridge builder
- Next step

- Old cycle new shift
- Bringer of the dawn
- Shape shifter
- Chameleon take on different form
- Bridge culture Continental Europe California
- Floating bridge
- Smooth connection - older generation and new
- See a new way of thinking without loosing essence of underpinning below
- Keeping clear boundaries
- Don't hold hands - encourage them to do what they need to do
- Basket, gathering resources for others
- Batwings
- Medicine presenter
- Crow/Hawk messenger
- A woman warrior
- The Reluctant Shaman

My life has taken on more and more of these qualities and my writing reflects the essence of what my life mission buddies pulled out of the air. See it's all there if we only can pay attention a little and learn to trust that space in between.

Ah yes, the trust thing, here she goes again, trying to send me out on a limb, with no safety net. One friend quipped I'm like the Rock of Gibraltar approach to personal development. What she meant was I shove you off the cliff. And see, you could fly, couldn't you? I knew that all along. So what am I doing in Sweden where it's the national skill to be reluctant and reticent and cautious? They've raised it to an art and it drives me nuts at times. That's why I like to write in English - few Swedes are interested in the Rock of Gibraltar approach, it's too scary for them and I don't hold their hand as they cautiously wait to see what the rest of the world will do. I digressed a bit there, gathered a bit of steam, emotional steam, useful as a locomotive to get things said or done.

I had to laugh when I saw The Reluctant Shaman description at the end of the list - it really fits. Only now I sneak it into my books. I find my type of energy works well in sharing thoughts in writing, it gives people a chance to digest what I say. When I speak live there isn't the delay, the cause for pause, and sometimes my ideas scare people. When the target stands right in front of you it's easy to shoot the messenger. So I rather like the cause for pause that the written or recorded word enables.

THE RELUCTANT SHAMAN

# Rest When Tired, Do When Inspired

Some people have very structured cycles and routines. Their bodies even seem to thrive on regularity. I'm not one of those people. Much of what I do is cyclical. Unless I have an appointment early in the morning, that means before ten o'clock, I won't set an alarm clock. I let myself sleep until I wake up. I eat when I'm hungry. I rest when I'm tired. I do when I'm inspired.

Nature has cycles. I suppose it's become more obvious living at a latitude like Alaska. Where winter days are short and dark and summer nights go on it seems like forever. It's natural to go inward as the darkness invades and slow down. As spring arrives, activity comes to life again and you actually get to see your neighbors.

My creativity is cyclical. You can't have marvelous thoughts all the time. In between there are some real duds. Lucky for you I don't write year round. To be really creative, I think, requires periods of uncreative time. The gathering of inspiration actually happens while nothing seems to be happening. During Z 2 A time and space.

When it comes, inspiration that is, grab it as if your life depended on it. Go for it. Even if it wakes you up at five o'clock in the morning, or keeps you up past bedtime. If I do when inspired, the work gets done much easier and quicker than if I push myself to do it when I don't feel like it.

Rest when tired. Allow yourself to let go. Pushing the energy just makes the work harder. It isn't always easy to feel into the natural flow, but with practice it gets easier. I struggle with impatience and have to keep reminding myself to focus on what is here in front of me, right now.

THE GATHERING OF INSPIRATION ACTUALLY HAPPENS
WHILE NOTHING SEEMS TO BE HAPPENING

I'm human. So are you.

Take note of your natural cycles. Take note of your way of being. Take note of what makes you function best. We are no longer in the industrial age where everything had to be structured for the assembly line. We are now in the network age, where it's more about connecting the dots than fitting into a set structure.

# How Does It Feel?

Geographical astrology and logical calculations aside, what counts is how it feels. When making decisions, it is paramount to consider how we feel about it. Many times we have to try it out for a bit, go a ways down the path, to know what and how we actually feel. You can't stand beside it and experience it in your head. You actually have to go there and do the experience.

When I left my home in Paradise, Sweden to move to Annecy, France I sold all my earthly belongings and packed up the car with the rest and took off. The journey turned out to be a two month walkabout by car in Europe. I had driven 700 kilometers to end up moving 11 kilometers.

- So you didn't need to go on that trip, was a common remark. You could have just moved and been done with it.

Actually, no. You can't get there by mind travel only. The package deal was to do the walkabout, with all the meetings, experiences and conclusions that came with it.

It also prepared me for the European Tour I did the year after. As requests for Eva Parties rolled in, I knew about how long it would take me to drive between stops. I had a good idea what the roads were like and how much traffic I might encounter. So I could give them realistic dates. It was amazing to see the whole tour come together by some unseen magic. It would not have happened that way had I not followed the Annecy thread.

# Life Task and True Work, Study, Play and Rest

Another useful tool from the Michael Teachings is the Life Task and The Four Pillars, also know as The Trues. While I was visiting Colorado, I was fortunate enough to get an updated Michael reading from channel Nancy Gordon.

I include the information here, as it helps to explain how and why I sort the way I do, and it shows yet one more way to help us understand our path here on earth.

**Life Task**

To bring truth to bear where possible.

**True Work**

Putting thought to work. Relates to the writing. Good Work.

**True Study**

Having access to information that benefits others.

**True Play**

Barefoot along a sandy beach. Catching sunbeams.

**True Rest**

Solitary activity. Connection with the Higher Self.

Understanding our life task and the trues help us understand our own idiosyncrasies. For example, my true study of having access to information that benefits others clarifies why I so often share information, that I think will be useful to oth-

ers. It's easy peasy for me, no effort really, and that is char-
acteristic of all the trues. It comes naturally to you. It's your
particular way to be in the world.

WE USE OUR TRUES TO ACCOMPLISH OUR LIFE TASK

The more we're in tune with our trues, the more we find
ways to use and express our trues in daily life. It's one more
way to align ourselves with our true path.

We use our trues to accomplish our life task. Each supports
the others. They synch together. For some of us it takes half
a lifetime or more before we get it. When we are engaged in
our trues we are absorbed, we become more connected to the
source. We become energized.

# An UN Period

A normal project flows in a natural direction. The Z 2 A period, on the other hand, is discontinuous. It appears there are lots of dots, but they are not necessarily connected. The thoughts skip, the activities gap, the emotions have no apparent logic.

UN-rest is common, swinging from boredom, doldrums, to high speed chaos. This is life in the UN period. It's as it should be. How in the world will something new be able to form, if there isn't an UN space where it can enter?

Hmm...

The UN's are important. Perhaps even more important than the DO's. It's from the UN's that the impulse forward comes.

Empty space is of course not really empty. It is full of possibilities, unlimited choice, paths and ideas. Tap into the UN and you may just become wise. Or full of it. Discrimination, the ability to sort, becomes even more critical as we learn to tap into the UN. What is key? What is next? What feels like it feeds my soul? Now, in this moment?

Living moment to moment in a planned world is not easy. I have not mastered the task, as I'm sure you've already observed. But by letting each thing or thought have its due, I move forward, in my own way. The movement may not be movement, more an awareness, that life trudges on, even when it appears to be standing still.

Here in Sweden, in the November darkness, that inward

withdrawal, slowing down, hibernating impulse makes itself known. The bare trees against a winter sky, stillness, you can almost smell the approaching snow in the air.

Soon...

With candles lit, we sit by our windows and gaze at the snow falling gently, so quietly, outside.

IT'S FROM THE UN'S
THAT THE IMPULSE FORWARD COMES

# RE-Evaluate, RE-Member, RE-Think, RE-Consider

Before we can move forward into something new, it is appropriate to pause and do the RE-words.

RE-Evaluate what has worked and what hasn't. How did it feel? Did it work? Did I get the results I wanted? Have I learned something? Just because something was the right thing to do last year, doesn't mean it still fits. Stopping to review and reevaluate is necessary for progress. Life is so much about change and growth, well at least for me. If anything defines the Z 2 A period it is just that, the time to reflect. To pause. To let the thoughts drift and meander.

RE-Member where you have been. Maybe this is why we pull out the pile of photos that have started to gather dust, and finally take the time to go through them. We sort and put the pictures into albums. We share them with friends. While we do this we remember what was. All this helps us in getting a perspective on where we have been, what we have done, and perhaps a glimmer of insight into what we may want to change for the future.

RE-Think your options. Turn them around. Try to look at things from another perspective. Rethink your approach. There are many ways to accomplish the same things. I've been looking at my marketing strategy for my books and services. The last few years I have done some pretty extensive tours, doing talks and book signings for small groups. It's been a lot of fun and has satisfied my travel urge, but they take a lot of time and effort to organize. Maybe I would rather focus on fairs for a bit. In a few days of intense work, I get to meet more people than I do on my tours. It's still on the rethink list, but already I am booking fairs, having just signed up for the London Book Fair and the Harmony Expo in Stockholm in the spring. In the next few years, I may want to spend more time writing and doing seminars than travel to do small presentations.

RE-Consider your options. Allow yourself to think outside the box, to look at alternatives on the opposite side of where you are. This is essential at mid life, when many people switch sides, so to speak. It's time to explore the other side of the street. The stay at home Mom goes back to school or starts a business. The hard driving executive starts to explore the softer side. Counselors and therapists all of a sudden take a year or two off to study computer science. Or the engineer switches career and becomes a healer.

Life has handed us a space, a stop, a pause, an ending for a reason. Whether it's an illness, a move, a job that's ended or a relationship gone sour doesn't really matter. The abrupt, or soft, demise of what has been is a signal that a Z 2 A period has landed in your life. Take advantage of it. Stop, pause and reflect, before charging ahead to rebuild what was.

Many years ago a friend of mine was laid up with a concussion for a few months. She said it felt like her brain was being rebuilt, kind of like a computer. I asked what changes were being programmed into her new brain.

- Oh no, my brain is being rebuilt just like it was, she quipped.

There was no room for even discussing the possibility that maybe, just maybe, the concussion was there for the very purpose so she could consider other ways to see the world, like an opening to change her consciousness. To get a new lease on life. Just because you are handed an opportunity to change, does not mean you take it.

Another friend was in a very serious car accident, that also brought chaos to the brain. Ten years after the accident, she's a totally different person. She chose to allow the change in consciousness, to allow a new her to emerge. She's softer yet stronger, more creative and more in tune with the world. The journey was not an easy one, yet she has no regrets. She was done being the old her. As a healer she's gained incredible insight into how the life energy builds a new structure from the ground up.

RE-THINK YOUR OPTIONS

# Not Yet

Not yet, has got to be the ultimate Z 2 A expression. Waiting. Biding your time. It's not ready. All the pieces aren't in place yet.

My psychic friend stopped by the other day. The one who sees me moving to the US. Every time she talks to me she sees container ships, crossing the ocean.

- Not yet, she said. I see you tying up loose ends, like you are tying ribbons on all these bags. One by one, you are preparing. When the time comes, it will move swiftly. Then all the groundwork will be laid.

I already knew it wasn't yet. My inner guidance in meditation showed me that writing this book is next, and that is all I need to know right now. I've often wondered what the value is in knowing that you will be moving on. In a way, nothing lasts. Eventually we all die, or move on.

This is not the first time I've been told that I would be moving, only to go through a very long waiting period. So does it help? I'm not sure. Would I live differently if I knew I was staying here? Does knowing there is change in the air (when isn't there, in my life) help me live better, here in this moment?

In Z 2 A time doesn't exist, so how come it feels like waiting? It all comes back to 'now I do this, now I do that' and as I go along I live and learn. Life goes on. What is a bit tricky is relating to what is around me, knowing I'm about to pull up the stakes. But you can't sit with your bags packed for several years. I've experienced frustration in being told this is what is around the corner, only to discover the corner is a VERY long ways away. Or that corner doesn't arrive. The prediction isn't even correct.

You can't predict exactly. The future is dependent on all of us, on all the decisions that we make. So when someone sees a future, they are seeing the most likely future. And the folks over there, or up there, or wherever the bodiless entities hang out, are notoriously poor in giving time coordinates, since to them all is now. Of all the predictions I've heard over the years from psychics, very few have been right on.

One was from a friend of mine who very occasionally gets a message. In all the years I've known her she's given me two predictions. The first one she was right on.

She saw me moving to France and that it would be very important that I know the nuances of the language. At the time I was in the corporate world working in the USA. It was a totally off the wall prediction as our company had no presence in France. A year later I became the on-site Purchasing Manager for the construction of a new factory in Orléans, France. Learning the language turned out to be key in our success.

The second prediction is still out there waiting to be fulfilled. She said 'I don't know when, I don't know how, but you have an absolute bestseller in you.'

We'll see. When the doubts creep in, it helps me keep on writing.

Not yet.

NOT YET

# Snow Fairies

I'd like to tell you about snow fairies. I think they are like Devas, only they are in charge of snow. Years ago in a reading with a psychic snow fairies showed up.

- What's with all these snow fairies? she asked. They are all around you. Do you like snow?

- Yes, I love snow, I replied. That's what I miss the most about Sweden. The crunchy sound under your boots, the quiet when the flakes float through the air. The stillness of winter. The clear air. The sparkling snow in sunlight or on a starry night. It's beautiful.

- Well these snow fairies are calling to you, says the psychic.

It took quite a few years before I ended up here, in snow country. In the beginning, I was so excited when winter arrived. I don't get quite as excited now. There are some practicalities like hazardous driving and shoveling snow, not to mention the short days.

But this year I'm liking the snow. Maybe the snow fairies are here, helping me write. On the other hand, winter has just started. I was born in early December so maybe it's more natural for me to like snow. I'm a bit contrary, most Swedes love summers here and wouldn't miss it for the world. It's when a lot of the expats come home.

I think summers here are too cold and definitely too short. I'd happily live on a sunny sandy beach most of the time and come to winterland a few months. To hibernate and go inward. A natural Z 2 A environment. Dream time. Creative time. Stare into space time. Meditate on the snow fairies. They play and dance as the flakes flurry. Freely networked, each flake unique.

When I lived in the country, my neighbor dragged me out on full moon nights, when the skies were clear, to go walk in the forest. It was magical, the moon lighting up the snow, the tall dark firs, the frozen lake. The smell of snow. Clean. The tracks of a moose, or deer. We might see a rabbit or a fox. Magical moonlit nights. Bundle up and trudge out to be blessed by nature.

To be truthful, I think I can wax lyrical about nature no matter its state. As long as it is nature. I'm definitely not a city person. I went gaga over the colors in Colorado. Incredible, fantastic colors.

As this book has been so many years in the writing, I can report that each year, I get less and less lyrical about snow. Long before I returned to Sweden, I started buying fuzzy sweaters and warm clothes. My intuition was guiding me to start collecting wear for the climate.

I've stopped buying winter clothes. For some time now I can't seem to get enough summer clothes, shorts and dresses, for a balmy climate. There's no logic in that. Our summers last maybe six weeks. Perhaps I'll find that sandy beach where the trade winds blow?

However, not yet. There is a balance between dreaming and letting intuition seed the future with living here now. We need to participate in the life we have right now, in this moment. Do what is before us to do, at this point in time. To savor what we have.

# I Had a Plan, God Had Another Plan

The best laid plans do occasionally have to be altered. I had intended to spend the fall and winter writing this book, so that it would be ready in time for the London Book Fair.

Yes, I had a plan. It turns out God had another plan. So, guess what? My plan is altered.

YOU CAN'T FORCE YOUR WILL ON THE UNIVERSE

This fall, instead of having plenty of space for writing, has been full of parental issues. I am the only sibling here to help them out, and I've spent the last few months moving them into assisted living. I thought I was done, but there is more.

I realized the other day there is no way I'll be able to complete enough of Z 2 A to make it a viable showpiece at the London event in mid April. On the other hand, I have been meaning to revamp *The Naked Truth - an exercise in therapeutic storytelling and the principles involved in becoming finally free*, published by Author House in 2003. There are all kinds of business reasons to publish it on my own label Divine Design. But more importantly, the book needs to be updated and expanded, and retitled. What started as an exercise for my own therapy turned out to be a page turner more thrilling than real life. I've learned a lot with every book I've published.

It's funny, creative stuff is rarely logical one-two-three. It often feels disconnected. But in the end the Divine plan always works best. I have noticed an incredible Divine synchronicity in all that's been happening around my parents. I'm not surprised really that I get to revamp *The Naked Truth* now. I need to write about all that has been happening and that book is the perfect venue, making it even better than the first time around. The second edition has a new name *Secrets of Transformation*. It's about one third longer than the original edition.

We live and learn. Might as well roll with the punches. Put another way, you can't force your will on the universe.

# Change of Plans

Bobbing and weaving through inputs, ideas and ponderings on the road to where? Going back a ways, you may recall I got a message to start a healing center in Hawaii? First I checked out the big island, appropriately enough called Hawaii. I had a nice time, but felt it was not my island. This spring I decided to revisit Kauai, the retreat island. I'd spent two weeks there nineteen years ago. I didn't speak to a soul the whole time I was there. Talk about Z 2 A energy!

KUAI IS Z 2 A ENERGY

Tickets and condo booked, I'm curious what I shall find this time. Right before my trip, I have a dream. A therapist colleague from the Shen world clearly says 'change of plans.' Then I wake up. This colleague just happens to live on the islands. My first thought is that the plan to start a healing center in Hawaii is changed, that something else is in the offing.

I have no idea if the change has to do with the course that the United States is taking or if it's on a more personal level. Plans change, what looked like a good course can alter as we mosey on down the road. Either way, I had a nice relaxing time on Kauai. I was not stirred to move there. It could be that my guides simply wanted me to visit the island for the energy. That I simply needed to go there for a bit. During my excursion to the Botanical Gardens I felt strong waves of grief for two of my friends who'd passed over. Both were very connected to flowers. One of them had her ashes scattered on Hawaii, which island I don't know.

Now I'm back home in Sweden and feeling pretty content. This is a pretty good place to live and things are opening up on the home front. I've had two art exhibits this summer, my Swedish books are selling well and the inquiries keep dropping in for courses. And the Swedish economy is doing fairly well compared to the rest of the world. I'm reminded how much work is involved in a major move as a friend copes with settling in a new place across the country. Maybe I don't need to do that again? I already have that experience. Or maybe not yet is the operative word.

# Clarity

These days, I rarely consult psychics or channels, preferring to intuit the information myself. But every once in a while a check in with the unseen planes is good to do. I was confused about all the various dreams of places I'd like to live, as they kept changing and were quite different as to climate and experience. Then there was my psychic friend who saw me moving back to the States, lock stock and barrel. What was she seeing? And from time to time, friends or perfect strangers would see me living in Australia, New Zeeland, Spain, France, Italy or Egypt. I've got my own vision of a rose cottage in England. And a villa on the sea somewhere. Who was right? What did the messages mean?

I booked a consultation with a channel I trust. Her guide came through with the following:

You don't have to move. You are at home wherever you put your feet down. You do need to travel, but it doesn't have to be far away.

What you yourself and intuitives or psychics pick up, are the various travels you've set up for yourself in this lifetime. This does not mean you have to move there, going to these places for a month or two or three is enough. You've set yourself up in this life to not have the kind of bindings that tie you down, so you could be free to come and go. You have many people to meet and places to experience. You may go there to write and paint gathering inspiration from each experience.

Listen to your own inner guidance. How do you feel about it?

Never mind the opinion of others. Your psychic friend who sees you back in the US is picking up information about past incarnations. You do not need to physically revisit all those places.

Your parents have their own journey, their own time plan. You're not here to be tied down taking care of them. When the time comes and you are needed by their side, you will find it easy to do so.

With a sigh of relief, I understood the messages. So many times, we get images via the intuition, but it's in the interpretation that the true gem lies. Many times, the interpretation becomes clear quite a ways down the road. Until then, it's easy to bark up the wrong tree.

IT'S IN THE INTERPRETATION THAT THE TRUE GEM LIES

# Crashed Dreams

I was surprised at how relieved I was that I didn't have to move. Since my departure from the corporate world almost twenty years ago, I've been mostly in a Z 2 A space. Looking forward to settling in.

Then a wave of emotion came crashing in. Followed by more waves. Time to grieve all my crashed dreams. As I had seen images of myself living in a rose cottage in the UK, doing a healing center in Hawaii, living in a garden paradise on the Mediterranean, emigrating to New Zealand, I felt sad that these dreams were not to be. I was staying right here in Sweden. For now.

Logic has nothing to do with it. A natural part of the process is to grieve those paths not taken, whether or not we actually would have wanted to go down those paths. We still need to grieve that which is not to be in this lifetime.

I can hear you wonder, won't you still be able to experience those places? Well yes, but not in the way I had pictured, and I felt sad, very sad. Best not to analyze the feelings, just have them, let them out. It's a bit like cleaning out a closet, or clearing the cobwebs. Once the emotions are let go of that belong to the past, you can get on with a new future.

Spending a few days going within to bawl your eyes out does wonders. As you might have gathered, this is an on going process throughout life. As the wrecks of my old way of seeing the world dissipated, new possibilities started to emerge.

# Time to Explore

With clarity in hand and a bagful of emotions chucked, I started looking around for bigger quarters. A new sense of settling in descended on me. I realized how many connections I'd made in the ten years I'd been hanging out here between my travels.

I checked out rentals, went looking at open houses, wandered the neighborhoods, made lists of what I wanted, and dreamed. As we explore, we gather information and gain clarity of what feels good and what doesn't. Looking at houses for sale I learned about the market, how things work, what to look out for, and pretty soon had a realistic idea of what I could afford.

I've already done the bit of refurbishing houses when I was a landlord so I wasn't keen on a fixer upper. I have too many books to write, too much art to create to be spending my time redoing a house. I looked at building a house from scratch, but quickly realized that was way beyond my budget.

Synchronicity is an interesting thing. My neighbor had gone with me to another town to look at factory built houses. On the way home she asks if I've been to see the new row houses built in town. No, I hadn't. I didn't like the colors on the outside and they were price wise out of my league. At least go look says my neighbor.

Funny thing, the next week there is an ad in the paper that those very houses are open for viewing on the weekend. I mosey on up there. The insides are airy and modern, very nice. I spend a long time talking to the agent, but in my heart I know I can't afford this.

Monday the phone rings. It's the real estate agent. She has a buyer for one of the units, but they need to sell their house. She thought of me. This house is totally refurbished: new kitchen with the latest appliances, bathrooms redone, new washer/dryer, new wallpaper, they just repainted the outside, new deck and fences in the back yard. Like a new house in a well maintained neighborhood. And it's 1300 square feet. Sounds too good to be true. I go look and say yes. The bedroom even has purple wallpaper, my favorite color!

Then emotions come again. Whenever we step into a new energy, the old crap comes up to be let out. We're not meant to take it with us, but to let it out when the time comes. All emotions are allowed!

First I am really excited. A place of my own. I've been renting or living in other people's homes for almost twenty years. This felt big. A relief. Then fear, am I doing the right thing? Am I ready to be a homeowner and deal with all the maintenance myself? You get spoiled renting, just call the landlord when there is a problem. On the other hand, I can do whatever I want since the house is mine.

In my apartment I've been catching up on routine stuff, like cleaning the windows. The time had come to unclog the bathtub drain. Now what does clogged drains have to do with Z 2 A? Everything. Symbolically, I need to clear out the old muck, to move into the new. At the same time, emotions overwhelm me. I cry and cry. For all my lost dreams. I remember how scared to death I had been to leave my corporate job in France, how terrifying it had been to leave that safe structure. Now I'm moving into a more structured existence and I'm just as terrified. Massive tears flow as I let go of deep stuff from so long ago. When I was being nudged to depart from my corporate safety net, I froze up, totally constipated until I decided to let go. Now, I throw up, literally spewing out all the old crap, the old emotions, the lost dreams.

WHENEVER WE STEP INTO A NEW ENERGY, THE OLD CRAP COMES UP TO BE LET OUT. WE'RE NOT MEANT TO TAKE IT WITH US, BUT TO LET IT OUT WHEN THE TIME COMES. ALL EMOTIONS ARE ALLOWED!

I never cease to be amazed at the treasures tucked away in

our bodies, ready to clear when the time is ripe. The clogged drain also tells me it was time to get on with writing again. This book has been idle for many months, and wants to be finished now. Feels appropriate to complete before I move in about three months time. While I am still in the space between. All the notes are there, I just haven't fleshed them out yet.

You might have guessed already that the book didn't get finished before I moved. I've been in the house two years, and now finally I get to complete it. 2011 is a Z 2 A year so appropriately the universe made me delay until it was time.

# When a Door Opens

When a door opens, I walk through it. My mind may have a totally different idea of what is meant to happen right then, but what does it know? When I was guided to a house that was obviously meant for me, I did have a choice. I could accept that the universe sees farther than I, or I could insist it be my way or the highway.

It's weird in a way. Since I moved in here, so many people have asked me about the house.

- How is it? they ask, expecting abundant enthusiasm.

- It's fine, I reply. I do feel at home in the house. It feels totally mine. But is it what I dreamt of? No. But this is where I need to be, right now. I don't know how to explain the lack of gushing superlatives about my abode, and it's hard to put my finger on the feelings I have about it. Granted this isn't my first house, so that newness, like buying a new car, isn't there. On the other hand, when I think of the cars I've owned over the years, I've absolutely loved some, hated some, and been pretty indifferent to others. It's life I guess. Some experiences touch us deeply, others do not. Maybe the Buddhists have the right idea, learn to accept everything and not label it good or bad?

The car I have at the moment, is my favorite of all time. I love this car more than any other I've owned or driven. Why? I don't know. How can you explain feelings? They just are.

When a door opens, you may wonder what will happen if you were to walk through it. The only way you can find out is to take that step and do it. You won't know by traveling there in your mind, although it can give you a hint. Will you feel fear? Most likely. We all have fear of the unknown. I have it. You have it. We all have it. While sharing some of the adventures of my life with a new friend, she wonders if I don't ever get ever scared. Of course I do. Often. But I do it anyway.

Such is the path of the seeker. You don't know what is around the corner. You may fear that uncertainty, but you have to go there anyway.

WHEN A DOOR OPENS, YOU MAY WONDER WHAT WILL
HAPPEN IF YOU WERE TO WALK THROUGH IT

Every so often, I run into someone who has defined how their solution will look, complete with all the details. There is a potential trap in being this specific. It's easy to get locked into that mental prison that says my way or the highway. By being locked in to 'this is how it has to look to be right' we may miss the door that flies open, that actually is right for us, at that moment.

- I don't know what I don't know, says a friend of mine. It's the conclusion she came to after studying metaphysics for twenty years. The more we learn, the less we know. I can look back at my insights and conclusions and see that I was only partially right.

# In this Moment

'In this moment' is an exercise I learned early on, from favorite teacher insui. All of us in the group were in various states of confusion. Life as we knew it and expected it to be had gone bye bye. The rug had been pulled out from under us in various ways. Divorces, job losses and health issues were forcing us to learn new ways of relating to the world. Every once in a while one or more of us would surface a worry about the future.

– How am I going to survive financially?
– Will I ever have the energy to get back to work?
– What in the world am I going to do when my money runs out?
– What will happen if I can't ever get a job again?
– What if my health never gets better?

And on and on and on. We were all worried about the future. Many of us were trying to get back to where we were. Human nature, to try to get back that which is lost. But you can't move forward with all the past as baggage. Anyway, insui had this exercise for us. It's so easy. Three simple questions:

– In this moment, do you have food to eat?
– In this moment, do you have a roof over your head?
– In this moment, do you have clothes on your back?

We were OK. The answer to all of the above was YES. In this moment I am OK. That is all you need to know.

# Saving for the Future

Sometimes we have the means to fund our new life, but we think we need to hang on to it. Save it for retirement. Save it for a rainy day. Perhaps that day is here?

I've had many discontinuances in my life. Perhaps the universe thought I should have more practice than most, so I'd know what I was talking about in writing this book.

After my career screeched to a halt, I found myself back in Seattle with a paid off mortgage on my condo. I could live really cheap. But as life would have it, in order to grow I needed to move on. Was I scared? You bet!

It didn't happen right away. I spent several years in personal development workshops to get to the point where the universe meant I was ready. Looking back, there was so little I understood about my path. I didn't have a road map. I just had to learn to trust, and that didn't come easy.

Once the condo sold, I had a bunch of cash to put in the bank. Scary to me. What do I do with it? How do I handle it? Never in my wildest dreams did I think the universe meant for me to spend it. I thought I'd be back in the working world. Ha!

Long and the short of it, the money supported me through trips, travels, workshops and experiences. In a way it's too bad I didn't know this is what was intended. If I had trusted my intuition earlier, I would have chucked the logical path out the window and traveled a different path. I was going to write I would have ARRIVED sooner, but the point of the game is to go have the experience. If I had listened to that quiet intuition,

I wouldn't have done a nine month walkabout in Sweden, interviewing with all the top companies. It's now that I write about it that I realize I wouldn't be me without that experience. So what may look like a long way to get from here to there, is actually the path that takes us into ourselves.

Funny, this theme surfaced in my morning meditation. I was frustrated at all the 'interruptions' in getting to write this book. At the same time I acknowledged that the interruptions were part of the process, for some reason. Although I could feel that all the other stuff was keeping me from writing, it's somehow necessary for the book to become whole.

## FOLLOW THE PATH OF INTUITION IN ITTY BITTY STEPS

Not long after I had started writing books, money worries loomed on the horizon. I'd used up my condo cash and was loathe to tap into my pension savings. I needed to save it for retirement, didn't I? Besides, there was a 10% penalty for withdrawing the money at such an early age. I fretted. My friends listened to my ramblings. One of them turned out to be very wise.

- Maybe you have this money, because you are meant to use it, she said. If you use the money now, you will be free to focus on writing and creating. You won't have to take some job just to support yourself, which also would take time away from your writing. And if you do the writing now, you'll probably have enough royalties when you do retire.

I had the guts to listen to her. She was so right! I had the money because I was meant to use it, at that point in time. I started withdrawing on my pension IRA, paying the 10% penalty tax, and focused on writing. I am really glad for my friend's wisdom.

If you've sold a house or had a windfall for whatever reason, be smart and use the money to follow your heart. I see so many people trying to force a way to make money, when all they'd have to do is use what they got and follow the path of intuition in itty bitty steps.

# Disruptions

Anytime we loose our footing we enter Z 2 A space. When your computer or car breaks down, your cell phone goes on holiday, you lose a job, or move, or even take a trip. You break the pattern. There is an opportunity for something else to come in. There is a possibility of magic, a new experience, a new way of seeing the world.

I went off on a long trip to the states. On the way to the airport, my car broke down. My reliable Skoda that I'd had for nine years with no problems, got sick. The cooling system red light went on, it was no go. Up to now, this car had been running like clockwork. Just fill it up with gas, wash it now and then, service it when indicated, and just drive. Heaven. Now my baby was sick.

But, since I'd been a good girl and serviced it at authorized garages, I had the mobility guarantee. If, in the unlikely event my Skoda would break down, there was a toll free number to call and they would come to the rescue. They sent a tow truck and fixed me up with a one way rental to the airport. No charge. My car is in the shop being fixed while I'm off on my trip. Magic. Angels.

I must admit I was shook up. I had become so accustomed to the car being absolutely reliable, that a break down wasn't even in my imagination. A shake up is good for state of mind. It helps you see things in a different perspective. I experienced such gratitude when they told me not to worry about how to get on with my trip, they were setting that up, right now. My mind had been frantic about how to get on a train with luggage and all sorts of worries, and in one fell swoop it was all taken care of. Like magic.

Think of it as training for trusting the universe. It will be taken care of. The solution will appear. The path forward will come. A door will open. You will make new connections. But probably not like you had thought. Our minds are such prisons of how things should be. We need help to crack that armor from time to time. To let go and trust that as we mosey along, it will be all right.

When I arrived in Seattle, new problems arose. I couldn't get a signal on my mobile phone. Weird, I thought. I went outside. Nada. I set the find network to manual. Nothing. Then it dawned on me. I had switched phones since my last trip. Aw shit. I forgot to make sure it was a quad band gsm. All this one had, apparently, were the two European gsm frequencies. Crappola. Luckily, I had some AT&T phone cards, and at the airport they still have phone booths. I needed to call my friend who was to pick me up. She was not at baggage claim as we had agreed. Turns out she was down with the flu, and had sent me a text. Which I didn't get because my cell phone couldn't get a signal.

Off I went to get a Shuttle Express. During the ride north the driver and fellow passenger talked of travels far and wide. A wonderful glimpse of other ways to see the world. Which I would have missed if my friend had come to pick me up. There are opportunities in every discontinuity. We just have to be open for them.

# When You Least Expect It

Z 2 A is ever so much about the unexpected. New solutions. A different path. Seldom the one logic dictates. Not a straight line, but more a connect the dots experience where you have no idea what you are doing as you mosey from point to point.

My art is like that. Not only the way I paint, but also the way I'm showing it to the world.

When I started in Shen Therapy, I was encouraged to express my emotions without words, to paint what I was feeling. I poured my emotions into the vivid watercolors. It was fun as well as painful, tearful and exhilarating. The images were so full of what I couldn't express in words. Years passed in exploring all kinds of personal growth courses and groups. I got involved in meditation, sound healing, creative dance, therapy and massage.

Then Vedic Art came along. A course based on 17 principles, developed by Curt Källman and the Maharishi. After the basic course of four weekends, we continued to explore on our own, meeting one weekend a month. We had fun sharing techniques, talking about everything under the sun, exploring our love of color and expression together. I played with dry pastel crayons, with water color pencils, but most of all acrylic on canvas.

I never had a thought that I would do anything with my art. I just did it because it was fun. It met a need that I had. I didn't paint to produce anything. It took two years of Vedic Art before I completed a painting. All of a sudden, there it was. Wow, look, something I can frame. I was mighty proud to hang it on my wall. Signed by me.

Then another painting came together, and in a few years I had a small collection that hung on my walls. Intuitive art is so much about looking at it, meditating on it, being with it. First and foremost my art was for me.

I DIDN'T PAINT TO PRODUCE ANYTHING. IT TOOK TWO YEARS OF VEDIC ART BEFORE I COMPLETED A PAINTING.

After six years in the group, I felt a need to move on. Somehow you just know it's time. I needed something else, but what? There is often a vacuum in leaving the old before the new comes in. A waiting period. A what now? period. A testing this and testing that period. A fiddling around period. A non focused period. I painted some at home. I let it rest.

I gave away some of my art, to my favorite relatives. I applied to join the local gallery walk, more accurate gallery drive as in the boonies we aren't all packed in like sardines. A friend, a real artist, you know the kind with a formal art education and lots of stipends and awards, encouraged me to apply. You belong in this group, he said. You'd help elevate the quality, we need you. So I applied. Imagine my surprise when I got a rejection letter. Thanks, but no thanks. I couldn't believe it, nor understand it. It made no sense, but several of my friends remarked that I was meant to be doing something else. Mind you, not that whatever that something else is appears written in the sky. It can take time. It did.

A year or two passed. I applied again, encouraged by another artist friend, who does exquisite work. I thought surely this time I'll get in. No, I didn't. Funny thing is, this is not exactly the high art society. It's a bunch of locals who do a gallery drive one weekend in the spring. The quality is to say the least, variable. But no they did not want me. Boohoo. It hurt.

I found a new place to paint. In the summers, Vedic artists from all over the world congregate on Öland, an island in the Baltic Sea, to paint in barns. I was in hog heaven. Large easels, several of them, a cement floor you didn't have to mop if you spilled a drop of paint, and time. I spent two weeks the first summer and was amazed at what came pouring out. I'd brought some canvases that I'd started at home, that somehow came to fruition during those weeks. I came home and framed 26 pieces of art. My house was getting cramped for wall space.

A friend of a friend organized art exhibits at a café. I joined them for one show. It was fun but we sold very little. The café was a great place to hang out, but the clientele were unfortunately not in a financial position to buy. They were students, unemployed and recently arrived immigrants.

The shop where I'd get my art framed was opening a gallery to bring more people in. I did a show with them. Good exposure but that was about it. My neighbors liked my art. I'd bring my art to shows and fairs along with my books. I didn't sell any art, but got lots of spontaneous comments. People liked what I painted.

When my friend's sister was in the hospital with a boring poster to stare at, we replaced it with one of my paintings. She was in the last stages of cancer and kept my painting with her through the dying process.

A friend who is also an artist was getting requests for art she'd already sold. How could we make our art available so people could afford it? How could we make the same piece available to a larger audience? I thought a bit and the idea of a calendar popped into my head. This was December, so the logical thing to do was to plan it for the year after. The idea just wouldn't let go. So I set out to do a trial calendar. It came out in February. I sent it off to a few friends and connections. They were enthusiastic. Loved it. The sales were dismal, as could be expected. But that wasn't the point. I learned a lot. How to put one together. What people liked. What they asked about.

I contacted the hospital to see about exhibiting my art in their corridors. They declined. I was discouraged, again.

When summer comes, I go back to paint in the barns. I never know what to expect. Am I there just to be there or will something come out on the canvas? Sometimes it flows. Other times it's wild. I bring my music along so I can do creative dance and tone in my little apartment. It helps keep the energy flowing. I was so into it I didn't bother with brushes. Too slow. I played with glitter glues and alternated making a mess and creating really neat stuff. I made new friends, and felt quite at home nestled in with my creative buddies. We are so different in our expression and how we go about it, and that is exactly what it's about. Be yourself. Be unique. Indulge your you-ness.

SHE WAS IN THE LAST STAGES OF CANCER AND KEPT MY PAINTING WITH HER THROUGH THE DYING PROCESS

More and more art fills my walls. I take pictures and set up an art gallery online at Fine Art America, where you can order canvas and giclee reproductions as well as custom greeting cards.

Along came information about an event in India with

TellusArt. They would be doing workshops and exhibits with children and artists from Sweden and Asia to raise awareness for protecting wildlife. I'd had some indications that India was in my path. So I thought why not, I can at least ask for the application. When I looked at the questions, my heart sank. Formal art education, was the first question. List of exhibits, the second. Experience working with children. I put the application aside. I thought there is no point. After all my earlier rejections, why would I even think of applying???

A true Eeyore moment.

Something made me revisit it and fill out the application. Higher guidance maybe. I sent it in and forgot about it.

A month later an email arrives from TellusArt. They had completed the selection process. At first I didn't understand what it said.

- You are one of the fifteen Swedish artists selected to go on this trip.

I had to reread the email a number of times before my brain registered. I'm going to India! They picked me! It's such a joke. I can't get onto the local scene, but India, no problem. We start with an exhibit at the Prince of Wales Museum in Mumbai. One of the most prestigious places in the world to hang your art.

So the whole roundabout point of this chapter is to keep trying. Keep testing. Fling logic aside. And when you least expect it, a door will open and your job is to step through it. Don't back down. Go forward, even if you don't feel up to the task. The universe wouldn't be opening the door if you weren't meant to be there.

Painted in the gardens of The Prince of Wales
Museum in Mumbai during fusion workshop
with Scandinavian and Asian artists
for TellusArt

# Life Is a Treasure Hunt

A challenge in hanging out in the space in between is that you can't see the goal. The weaver in charge points you in different directions or feeds you inspiration, but there is no goal in sight. The path is the goal. Or as one of my favorite teachers used to say:

## LIFE IS A TREASURE HUNT

If we can approach life with the curiosity of the explorer, with the unwavering observation of a detective, or with the playful attitude of a child, then we truly are in the adventure of life.

We get this programming that we have to have goals. We have to know where we are going. We have to be profit oriented. We have to be something. I've had tremendous difficulty answering the question 'what do you do?' I've searched my childhood for clues, I've pestered friends and relatives to remember what I wanted to be when I grew up. They can't remember that I ever expressed a specific career goal.

Probably because I am a dreamer. When I was in High School the dilemma appeared as well. 'What are your plans when you graduate?' Horrible question. I hadn't given it a thought and hadn't a clue. 'Go on to college I guess' was my standard answer.

I did apply to the University of Washington, got in and the pragmatic person in me had by then appeared. I checked out what I could study and what kind of work I could get afterwards. With my straight A's in math it was either mathematics or engineering. I didn't want to be a teacher or statistician so I became an engineer, and made good money while it lasted. Had the computer industry been what it is today I probably would have gone that route. At the time you had to be an absolutely obsessed programmer to fit in. You've probably gathered by now that I live life in the slow lane.

It's not that I don't work hard, I do. My work comes in spurts, in rotes, in wholes, and in between it can look like I am the laziest bum in the world. But my method works for me and that is what counts. On the whole it's a productive way to work.

LIFE IS A TREASURE HUNT

# There Is a Job for Everyone

I love my friends. One of them is a Taurus with her feet on the ground. Although she likes me a lot she doesn't necessarily understand me. She finds my lofty ideas hard to get a grasp on, as they tend to be loose and free. Not the cut and dried here now basics for living. My task is to seed new thought and it's not always easy to convey the new in an old format. As a matter of fact you can't do it the old way.

That's why my books are published the way they are. I'm free to write them the way I'm inspired by my inner guidance. There isn't an editor with a commercial focus dictating the flow. I remember when *The Celestine Prophecy* came out. I heard about it through word of mouth. It was self published by James Redfield. He had written a story that was truly inspired from higher guidance. The book literally flew out of the bookstores. He was given the task to write it down.

Once he became famous, the big book publisher bought him out. The next book about the *Tenth Insight* didn't have the energy of the first. To me it was obvious that the publisher had steered the process from a left brain profit perspective. The story wasn't alive like in the first book. Sure it covered a lot of concepts. But you could tell that the authors natural flow had been tampered with. It was the last of his books I bought.

After my Taurean friend had read my book *The Pathfinder Process*, exploring organizations and relationships, with instructions like 'take what you need and leave the rest,' she still couldn't get her head around what I was trying to convey.

Being a mental and logical person, she felt that asking for an answer in meditation would be useful, but smart as she is, she asked to be given a symbol. She thought, 'in a symbol my intellectual brain won't be inclined to question what I get.' She was absolutely astounded when a hippopotamus showed up. Never in a million years would she have associated that image with me.

Surfing the internet for symbolic meanings she came across a site on ancient Egyptian symbols. The female hippo was revered as a goddess of fertility, transformation through death and rebirth, a protector associated with the northern sky. She represents tremendous power of an earthly and feminine nature.

I was reminded of a television program about women entering the priesthood. There was one woman in particular who recalled a vivid dream she had the night before being ordained. In it she was a pregnant hippopotamus standing in front of a well. She bent down into it and drank deeply. As she brought her head back up she was snorting water and air, there was an incredible sense of deep connectedness with the mother goddess, the feminine powerful aspect of earth. She described it as a feeling of being in heat, as in fertile, full of sexual excitement and empowerment.

The hippo also represents deep emotions, that are under the surface, and the possibility of transforming these undercurrents in a feminine powerful way.

We who are given the task to seed the new, are doing it on the inspiration axis. A book about the space in between can't and shouldn't be written or edited in the same manner as a commercial detective story or a spiritual how to book. To illustrate the flow, or beingness in the now, I have to be in that space and write it that way. Which is why the threads bob and weave. It is not a straight line progression from A to Z. We are hanging out in the void, the creative space, where the stars shine against an indigo sky.

We all have different tasks. Many years ago, on a stomachs

tour of Europe, we passed by Düsseldorf and lo and behold found the English bookstore. Just happened to meander right to it. There are no coincidences, right? I bought Bob Geldof's autobiography *Is That It?* about how he came to be the instigator and organizer of Live Aid.

As he describes it, God came knocking on his door. A scruffy Irishman answered. God says 'you'll do' and Live Aid came into being. Bob had watched the drought disaster in Ethiopia and somewhere he felt the pull to do something. He answered God's call. We all get called in one way or another. Our circumstances, skills, connections and development needs all play into what we are called to do. But in every case, the task you are given is one that is uniquely yours to do. No one else can give it the touch that you can.

MY TASK IS TO SEED NEW THOUGHT

# Life without Television

One way to make room for a space in between, is to unplug yourself from habitual structures and activities. In writing this book I am changing my patterns. Instead of getting up, doing my exercises, meditating and eating - I may start writing as soon as I get up. Or I turn it around. I write in the spaces in between. In most lives you have to start by creating those spaces.

I'm old enough to remember life before television. You can unplug the TV. Do you have any idea how many hours you spend in front of it? Have you reflected on what you get out of it? Does it feed your soul?

A few years ago I visited some friends in Germany. I really liked being in their house. After a few days I noticed I hadn't seen a TV. First I thought they had it in a study or something. Curious as I am, I asked. Turns out they didn't have a TV and perhaps more amazing, they never had one. They read, listen to the radio and have so many activities and interests they never really missed it. It's like they never got started and then it wasn't important.

- But how about your kids? I asked. When they were growing up surely all their friends had TV?

- Yes, but once they got over the fact we didn't have a TV, they turned to more creative play, my friends replied. In fact, now that both of them are in their thirties, we can say that they are far more creative than their peers. So not having grown up with a TV was not a loss. It was a plus.

When I moved into town, I was in the same boat. Life without a TV. Sure, sometimes I missed having it to turn on, just to have something to watch. But as I check the newspapers I rarely see a program I really want to see. So it's not a big loss. I take the paper so I can keep up with the local news and get an overall feel for what is going on in the world. I like the peace and quiet. Silence is actually a nice space. If I want I can listen to the radio, there is good music and often many interesting discussions. The intelligence level seems to be higher on radio programs than on TV. I have no idea why this is.

Perhaps it's easier for me to go back to life without one. We didn't get a TV until I was in the 5th grade, and summers were spent in the country, in houses without electricity or in a camper, so even then there were long periods without TV.

The TV issue has been one of economics as well. When I moved into town, I started afresh, so I only wanted to bring into my life items I really wanted. If I get a TV, there is first of all the cost of the equipment, and since I live in Sweden there is a TV license to pay, yet another tax I could do without. Every time I pondered the TV decision, I thought, what else could I do with the money? There was always something else I'd rather spend it on. Like travel.

Without a TV I get out more. I go to the movies, read, sit quietly, dance around the living room or call my friends. There isn't the automatic turn on the tube after dinner and veg out. One of my friends came home one night and realized he was zapping through the channels as usual. His habit was to come home and land in front of the tube and there he'd be until bedtime. This time he got so disgusted by this useless habit, he realized in a flash how he was wasting away in front of the tube. The realization grabbed him so strongly he pitched the TV out of the window.

Wow, I thought, when he told me this. Quite a strong thing to do. He said he went without for a few years, then realized he missed watching movies, from videos and DVD, so he bought a new set. But his habit has changed, and I would say most importantly his awareness of where his time and energy is going has shifted. There is an awareness of spending time on activities that have a return on investment, in pure human terms.

Thinking about where our time goes, becoming aware of our patterns, makes us able to shift our behaviors, should we wish to do so. You don't have to be so drastic as to throw the TV out the window. But you can turn it off. For a week, a month, make a free TV day a week. It's your life and your choice. When you do, don't try to fill the space, not at first. Just be present with it, notice how you feel. Notice what your body says, what feelings and thoughts come up. Just observe. Later on you will feel prompted to take action, but the first step is observe. Contemplate. Be with it. Feel what it's like to have space. Discover what is hiding in your empty.

You can do the same thing with magazines, newspapers, the internet and catalogs. With anything you habitually do, you can break the pattern, to see if you want to change it. A first step can be to simply notice where your time goes. Most of us feel there is not enough time. To change that, you first have to become aware of where your time goes, then you can evaluate which activities feed your soul or are really necessary for your survival. Cleaning out your time closet is just as important as cleaning out your clothes closet or garage. You have to get the clutter out of the way to function well.

I spent a couple of years without a TV then some money landed in my lap and I bought a used little fattie with a built in VCR. My relationship to the boob tube is different after my hiatus. It's been fun to explore the new series and watching video movies. Eventually a DVD player found its way into my house. Gotta keep up with technology to some extent, or?

It's all about choice. Choosing to decide. Deciding to choose, as Michael would put it.

# Stepping into the Unknown

I don't know why we have been so trained to think that we have to know what is ahead, so we can plan. The future is uncertain, and it can't be predicted based on the past. The future is always a step into the unknown.

Nature gives us a clue. It has cycles of growth and rest. Natural processes such as forest fires and floods are in fact necessary for the rejuvenation of nature. We humans are much in the same boat. Sometimes it takes an 'earthquake' in our lives to make the change happen that is good for us.

In recent years there have been a disproportionate number of natural disasters, with great loss of property as well as human lives. In the short term, it's a catastrophe for the people involved, there is no denying that. But in the long run something good will come out of it. In every loss there is a gain. After the tsunami, there was more money donated to helping organizations than ever before. The whole world was involved. People realized they may not make it to retirement, that NOW is all we have and we can never know about tomorrow.

My dentist and his wife decided to sell their practice, take time off and re-chart their lives. They took the opportunity and altered their course in life. They had worked hard, but the stress was getting to them. Why not enjoy life while you can. Pause and reflect on what is important to you. If your job is killing you, who is going to thank you when you die? What is it you really want before you die? What is on your bucket list?

- When they close the lid on my coffin, I don't want to have any regrets, of things I didn't do, a friend of mine used to say. I don't want to go to my grave wondering what would have happened if I took the chance. I want to have taken the paths offered to me. I don't want to think I wish I had done this or that. I want to have done them. I want to have lived.

THE FUTURE IS ALWAYS A STEP INTO THE UNKNOWN

Very wise that friend of mine. I have often thought of his words as I've found myself at one crossroads or another.

- If I don't do this now, will I wonder later what would have happened if I had? I ask myself. If the answer is yes, I would always wonder, then I go ahead and do it, no matter how frightened I feel. The fear is really of the unknown. When I step into it, the fear dissipates and I find my footing again.

Not taking a step, resisting it, actually makes the fear increase. Eventually your body is all in pain because you are blocking the natural life energy flow in your body.

Some of you have objections because of money. You can't do thus and such because first you must have the financial security to live your dream. For a moment, just consider this. What if it's the other way around? What if the money comes when you step into your dream? What if the solution comes after you commit and take that first step? Well I can tell you that is how it is. It is futile to work to break your back at something you don't enjoy just to build a nest egg so you can do what you want.

The earlier you take the step into your dream, the easier it will be, the less backtracking you will have to do. The universe supports your stepping into the unknown. Do you think the explorers knew where they were going, what they would encounter? Of course not. I think we've lost that sense of adventure, that sense of excitement, of new discoveries, new horizons. We've become lethargic. I want to wake you up, reignite the playful child within you.

What you can do before you charge into the unknown is take stock of your financial situation. First order is to get out of debt, pay off all loans and credit cards. Align your outgo so it's less than your income. Evaluate where you spend your life energy, what return you get on your investment of time and money. Eliminate everything that doesn't feed your soul. Then start saving. Even the poorest family can scrape together enough money to pay for a funeral. My point is that when it really counts, you can find a lot more money that you think you have. When you live your dream, it may not cost nearly as much as living a high flying career, especially if it's not what you really want. For some, the high flying career is their life purpose, it is what they are meant to do. But if you have to drag yourself off to work every morning, spending your time dreaming about what you'll do when you retire, after work, on vacation - it's time for a change. Big change.

We've lost that sense of adventure

# Escape Velocity

I don't know why they teach us that life is about getting settled and finding one's niche and having a structure in one's life. Why? Is it about control? Is the fear that if we all got loose and creative we would start to think our own thoughts, learn to look at the world through a discriminating lens and discover the emperor has no clothes? Pretty close to the truth there I imagine.

The idea of controlling the masses is not new. If you want to tax and usurp people, you can't have them happy and heaven forbid, think independently. So most societal structures are built on keeping you under control.

Escape velocity, we used to call it, when I worked in the corporate world. The idea being that once you hit a certain speed you are beyond their reach, their grasp. It's impossible to control a truly free person.

What fascinates me are the number of leaders who have gained their inner freedom while imprisoned by their oppressors - Vaclav Havel, Benazir Bhutto, Anwar Sadat and Nelson Mandela to name just a few. You can't shut out or kill the light. And the more you suppress, the more darkness you try to impose, the stronger the light gets.

When the second Iraq war started we had a painting weekend. We were all a bit concerned that we'd be painting horrible war scenes with blood and guts. We are after all tuned into the greater energies in the world. That weekend we painted more light than ever before. It was as if the outbreak of the war freed up the light to come pouring in. It was truly amazing to see all the light work carried on as the carnage began, to realize that in the worst disaster there is the strongest light.

Likewise in the tsunami. There were so many souls departing at once, that it opened up a tremendous light portal. While a tragedy in human terms, there was rejoicing in the expanse of light available to us here on earth.

## ALLOW THE ANSWER TO UNFOLD IN ITS OWN SWEET TIME

This book is like no other I've written. It weaves and bobs, seemingly without structure, at times flowing along like a river, or a stream of consciousness. Which is exactly what it is. Shall be interesting to see how it all comes together. That is one of the points of hanging out in the space in between. Not knowing the outcome or how all the disparate pieces will fit together in the end. Trusting the process. Trusting that it will all come out all right. Doing for the sake of doing, without attachment to the outcome. In the end it could turn out the book is not a book at all but some diary I had to keep to get to the next level. The outcome may not at all be what I think it is meant to be.

Be still and wait on the will of heaven, is one of the Runes messages. I remember a period when I drew that card over and over. I wanted to move forward, but the Runes said now is not the time. Allow the answer to unfold in its own sweet time. The purpose of your doing could be so different from what you imagine. You'll only know by stepping onto the path.

# When Old Structures Crumble

- Is the emotional state connected to the physical state? my friend wondered after suffering from whiplash and burnout while also working through deep family issues.

- You bet, I answered.

When we have a physical trauma such as whiplash, or an emotional trauma such as dramatic loss, the body goes into shock. It's a protective mechanism. All but the essentials for survival are suppressed. Emotions and memory get shunted aside, to be dealt with at a more opportune time.

After a big loss it takes time to build the new energy system, to clear out the emotional and mental cobwebs and to learn new pathways. As emotional release occurs, or even physical for that matter, the skeletal structure of the body alters and the muscles need to adjust themselves to the new stance.

People who have experienced a loss seem so tender. They are more sensitive to others energies. Much of their own energy is directed inwards, focused on the inner. Which is why a person in transition needs lots of time alone. They are very busy on the inner planes.

This extended time of inner restructuring can be used to maximum advantage if one is willing to work with what comes up and can get past the initial resistance to change.

Organizations fall apart, or relationships, or bodies. These are ways we are led into the space in between. It's a marvelous opportunity to pause and reflect before charging ahead. To take stock of what was, explore what is in the moment, and discover a new way of living. Nature is change and so are we. Look at a landscape, over time, it changes. Trees grow up and die, volcanoes spew out lava and alter the entire ecosystem, earthquakes render the path impassable.

ACCEPT THAT THE OLD NO LONGER EXISTS

Don't just rush in to replace what you lost when your own life experiences an earthquake or flood. Stop and listen. Reflect. Go through the emotional stages of grief, shock and denial, anger and sadness, and emptiness. Allow the nothing to be there.

In my hiking group there is a woman who works at the Red Cross second hand store. She told me they often get newly widowed women volunteers, they are so wound up after their loss and don't know how to fill their time. So they rush out to find anything to keep them busy. Finding new activities is of course beneficial, but to try to plug the empty hole with frantic activity just keeps you from feeling your grief.

Oh I'd love to see the world understand the processes of life, this is what real consciousness is, the absolute presence in everything that you do. Think if we all had this awareness, if all societal structures were run with full consciousness, imagine how different the world would be. We would act from a deeper place of being, we would allow that which is no longer useful to slip away or fall apart. Even though perhaps painful, we would be able to let go of the old.

A house, if not build on solid ground, or not built well, can be repaired for a time. But eventually you have to tear it down and build a new house. The same applies to our lives and to any organization. There comes a time to let the old ways and structures go, to let them die a natural death, or to let the opportunity for change move in when disaster strikes. I think that is such an important lesson. But to get there you have to be able to allow death. To not feel that you have to save the old no matter what. You accept that the old no longer exists. Sure there is going to be a grief process. Sure it's going to hurt. But in the letting go of the old, you make room for the new.

To make the garden healthy, you have to weed and prune. Likewise in life and any organization. But with care and conscience. I'm not talking about the greed based reorganizations that have plagued us since the early 1980's. They have little to do with a natural process of death and rebirth, they are what a friend of mine christened the MBA cancer. In other words the bean counters have moved in to destroy that which the visionaries and philanthropists built. But in the overall I suppose it serves the greater purpose, because hierarchical organizations are of the past, the future is in egalitarian networks. The way I see it. I could be wrong. Or right. What kind of world do you want to be a part of and help create?

# The Fine Art of Staring into Space

A pop to the next level also known as magic hour with Michael. Every once in a while I attend chat room sessions with Michael students around the world, channeled by Shepherd Hoodwin. Michael works through him to answer general and personal questions and there is a lot of energy work inter-woven into the sessions. Generally the sessions are at 9 pm Pacific time, which means 4 am here in Sweden. To enable the European contingent to participate, they had scheduled this one for 11am Pacific time, perfect for me to sit down at the computer at 8pm on a Sunday evening here in Sweden.

Turns out the time frame not only benefited those of us in Europe, there were a number of Australians there in addition to the usual North American contingent. There is something quite awesome in being spread out across the globe and con-necting energetically, like a grid laid on Mother Earth. In the group there are a number of healers, channels and meditators which of course facilitates the energy work.

One of the questions that came up was on the wounding in the second chakra (also known as the sacral, or hara chakra). Historically women have been raped and violated and many women and also men carry the scars of those wounds in their bodies. If you consider the pillage and carnage that we've been exposed to through lifetime after lifetime, it would be surpris-ing to find it all clear down there.

Michael/Shepherd did a group healing with us that was powerful, to say the least. Toward the end of the session we popped through to another level, the energy was poignant and pregnant and continued to reverberate through me. Michael said:

'The key to healing this is forgiveness to all who have harmed you, and secondarily, all you have ever harmed, in this and all lives. This is not something that can be done overnight. It might take daily work for as long as a year. Forgiveness is not as easy as simply saying 'I forgive you.' It means going to the core of your pain and releasing it in the spirit of agape (love that is wholly selfless and spiritual).'

The healing takes place in that space in between, Z 2 A. The work is done in an energetically charged space. I could feel it when we all tuned in and the healing energy flowed through. A revealing experience. The second chakra connects us to Z 2 A space and time.

HEALING TAKES PLACE IN
THAT SPACE IN BETWEEN, Z 2 A

Following this extraordinary Michael chat session, I am in a different space. Fuzzy and focused at the same time, although not intellectually bright. A feeling of *I am*. I spent quite a bit of time practicing the fine art of staring into space. Sitting on the couch, feet on the ground, feeling very grounded as a matter of fact, a cup of tea in my hands, and just staring into space. Eyes open not really focused yet seeing and observing what is there. My eyes rest on my paintings, and I feel deep energies stirring in my womb, cleansed and healed at a new level.

Letting myself be with the energies. Letting them work through me. Not rushing about accomplishing anything. I know that when I give myself the time to follow the flow, not force anything, let my intellectual brain give it a rest, new solutions will appear. There is no sense in pushing something when the energy is not there. Just let it be. What a difficult time we humans have with that.

Curling up on the couch is also a means of engaging the staring into space energy. Letting yourself float and dream. Don't even have to be at home. You can do it on an airplane 30 thousand feet up in the air. I love to drift away when I listen to classical music, but that is a different kind of dreamy drifty, another level of fantasy land. The staring into space with open eyes is a different layer of consciousness. They are all useful. It's good to practice a variety of altered states.

Let go of the goal, and focus on now. Now for me is staring into space, this morning. Then all of a sudden, the impulse arises to write, to make a phone call, to take a walk, or whatever. Listening inward and letting the flow unfold. Learn to trust the process and the universe. When you let go the universe assists you for your highest good. Scheming and manipulating are not needed, because all that belongs to you by right of consciousness is already yours, it can't be taken away from you.

I think we've lost the ability to not do. When was the last time you caught yourself just staring into space? You know that empty look, unfocused, where you just hang in time. Airports, airplanes, trains, buses - anywhere you sit with someone else doing the driving or flying - are great places to practice staring into nothing. But what do we do today? We're surfing our laptops, listening to our iPods, talking on our cell phones.

I think we've forgotten what it's like to stare into space, just be, let the thoughts drift like soft clouds. Empty. No to do list. No time. No space. Unfocused gaze. No think. No feel. Just be.

For advanced staring into space, recline in a hammock or on the couch, lie down on the grass under a tree in summer, sink into your favorite chair and go unfocus. Allowing the 'nothing pauses' makes me more effective, my mind clearer. Why don't you try it? Do less, not more. Be effective. Being busy is not the same as being efficient. Practicing the empty stare will clear your mind. I promise. The Buddhists meditate with their eyes open.

# Uncertainty

## A JOURNEY INTO A SPACE WE HAVEN'T BEEN BEFORE

Went for a walk in the snow flurries. I feel so uncertain. What am I doing here? What is the point and where is that energy to write? As I walked and pondered this I realized that as I am writing a book about the space in between Z and A, I'm hanging out in that space. So the book can't unfold like a regular project. This is like an un project that will shape itself in an entirely different manner. I do find that I sit and write snippets, in between thoughts and meanderings, that the writing isn't the main focus, but that it comes in the spaces in between. So all is as it should be, albeit I have some discomfort with it.

That is always the case when we do something different. It is uncomfortable. It is unknown. It is a journey into a space we haven't been before. But this journey is necessary so that we can build a better world. I am a Pathfinder, I have to keep reminding myself that. As a pioneer I go where others haven't been, yet. I show the way. But I don't know the way until I walk it or do it. Stepping into uncertainty. Wobbly. Discomfort. Yet somewhere inside me I know it's OK. I know it will turn out somehow. Trust in the process.

Which doesn't equate to being high or happy all the time. It can be lethargic and slow like trying to navigate through molasses at times. Be with whatever energy is there.

# Breaking Patterns

On returning from my walk, there were a couple of messages from friends. Normally I'd be delighted to chat with them, but both are really wordy, so neither would be short conversations. At the moment the inspiration is flowing for this writing, so I focus on that. The space in between is the perfect place to break habitual patterns, to test new behaviors, to alter ones course. Sure I could take the time to return the phone calls from my friends. But I already know from experience that by the time I would be off the phone it would be time to eat or go to class and there would be no words written today. And this particular stream would be lost. You have to grab it when it comes or you lose it.

I'm sure you've all had a great thought and been certain it was so profound you'd remember it later. So you didn't write it down. Only later you can't for the life of you remember what that marvelous sentence was. Where did that creative idea fly off to? We have to grab it when it comes. If you stop too long the opportunity is lost.

Likewise with windows of opportunity. Certain chances or meetings come your way. If you say no too many times, the window closes. If you don't grab the chance the opportunity is lost. My snow fairies must be very busy today. They are feeding me lots of material so I just have to buckle down and write as fast as my little fingers will allow.

Remember how earlier in the day I was practicing the fine art of staring into space? And now there is a veritable flurry of words and thoughts and ideas and concepts. This often happens after we pause, the flow gets going in a gushing manner. It's really creative and the juices flow, like lava down the sides of a volcano.

## GUIDED BY YOUR INNER LIGHT

Bundle of joy you might call it. Nuggets of wisdom, flow of life, rich words and content. Then all of a sudden it stops. Like sudden rain or thunder. It happens, then it's over. If you get nothing else out of this book I hope you understand the ebb and flow of life. It is in no way a constant, of regular repetitive occurrences. It's alive like the cycles of nature. Observe nature and you can see what I mean. It can be still and calm or windy and stormy. It can be dry or wet, hot or cold. The leaves die off in the fall and the tree rests during winter. In the spring new growth appears that culminates in the fullness of summer.

We too have such cycles. I believe one of the reasons so many people get stressed is they are trying to live lives that are not in tune with their natural cycles. If we can tune in and learn when we are productive, when we are awake and when we get our best sleep, we would all do better. There is a popular belief that you have to get up early in the morning, otherwise the day is gone. Think on this - if your most creative time is in the evening or the night hours, what good will it do you to force yourself to get up early in the morning? All you'll succeed in doing is making yourself so tired you won't have the energy to be creative, to be in the flow, to be productive in whatever your mission is.

I'd say you would be violating spiritual law, if you knew you needed a certain cycle, it was within your power to follow it, and you didn't. Once you know, once you are aware, once you are conscious, you need to follow what you know, or you'll be breaking spiritual law. As long as you are unconscious it can't of course be expected of you to behave as if you were conscious. There is responsibility in becoming aware, in taking the steps onto the path. But the rewards are also there. You become more and more your true self, guided by your inner light. You cease to be jerked around by the outside world in the same way as before.

Certainly you will still be interacting with it, as we are spiritual beings here on earth learning to be human. But you will come at it from a different perspective, from a different viewpoint. If something happens that gets your goat, you'll delve inward to release the hurt, to heal the karmic knot, then your approach will change as well as your response. Instead of reacting, you'll be able to respond, from a more whole you.

# Flogging a Dead Horse

Lately I've talked to a number of people who appear to be stuck. They are fighting a cause that seems to have no end or resolution. They feel like no matter what they do they can't win. They are stuck in a labyrinth, going around and around, never finding the exit.

I used to be pretty good at flogging a dead horse, as my friends expressed it. I didn't have sense enough to know that the 'horse,' that is project, relationship or situation was finished. I hadn't yet learned to recognize when the energy of something had gone dead. I'm much better at it now. I stop much earlier. I know when to quit and shift my energies elsewhere. Most of the time.

The learning hasn't been smooth. I've not understood the signals from my higher self. Sometimes I've knowingly ignored the instructions. Luckily our spiritual guides are patient and they don't get the two by four out right away. But they will when we don't pay attention.

If you have an accident or fall or stumble or get really sick, chances are your higher self is trying to get your attention. To shift gears, to pause, to reflect, to shift your focus away from problems and digging yourself deeper into the ground. Time to shift your attention to what increases the life force, the stuff that makes your heart sing.

The interruption in your life is your opportunity to pause, to heal, then sally forth into uncharted waters. It's easy to get stuck in the healing phase. The 'I'm not ready yet' routine. The

'I need one more layer of education before...' excuse. The 'I need to figure out how to make money' diversion. Allow yourself to let go of your mental prison long enough to dip your toe in the magic waters of Z 2 A.

STUCK IN A LABYRINTH

# Delhi Fog

We've arisen before the crack of dawn to journey to Taj Mahal, some 250 kilometers from Delhi. My fellow passengers soon fall asleep. I'm sitting in the middle and quickly realize that with no neck rest, I'll get whiplash if I try to sleep as we bounce our way down the road. Besides, I am fascinated by our driver. How can he see anything? The fog is so incredibly thick, like pea soup, and you can barely see the road, let alone any traffic on the way. It boggles my mind how our driver can navigate so securely in this fog. He must have some other sense hooked up.

Our driver honks, and to our left, an unlit bicycle appears out of nowhere. How did our driver know he was there? I can't see a bloody thing. How on earth does he find the way? You can't even see the road signs. As we move along, I wonder that he is so secure in his driving. Like he knows and sees beyond what I can see and sense. Before the roundabout appears, he knows it's there. Before the back of a truck appears right in front of us, he slows down. He knows it's there.

As I ponder in awe, I'm struck by how Z 2 A this journey is. We keep edging forward, trusting that with every movement, we will be guided to the next. Our driver is clearly hooked in to that Z 2 A space. He trusts that he will be guided. He doesn't worry about the part he can't see - yet! He knows that each step of the way, he will have the information he needs, right in that moment. What a marvelous way for the universe to demonstrate navigating through the unknown.

# Illness

After traveling through India with TellusArt for close to a month, I come home with a nasty cold and cough. I haven't been this exhausted for years. Since I work out of my home I have the luxury, most of the time, to build in rest and relaxation so I won't get sick. It's worked pretty well. I get the occasional cold, and that is about it. I haven't been bed ridden with an illness for many years.

As I spend day after day in bed, with no energy to do anything but read and sleep, in between trying to cough my lungs out, I'm reminded what illnesses are for. Space in between. Well of course this needs to go in my book. We in the western world try to treat illness as something to be gotten over and suppressed as quickly as possible. But I think the universe creates these pauses for a different reason. To go deep into Z 2 A space.

Illness is a time out for the body and the mind. A time when we need to let go. A time to surrender to spacey mind. A time to let the body take care of business. A time to strengthen the immune system. As we fall deep into the netherlands, we connect with a deeper level of ourselves. A part that is probably necessary for our next step in the world.

I remember one time I was really ill, in the hospital with a nasty infection. They were feeding me three different kinds of antibiotics intravenously. I was off in some weird space. There was a painting in the room. Some dark, dreary image that was in no way helping me find the will to live. Instead I felt drawn to death. As I sunk deeper, I realized this was one of my decision points. Did I want to go on living, or just let go and die? It would have been easy to slip off the planet, the painting was clearly helping me in that direction. But did I want to? Was I finished in this lifetime? As I sunk into the darkness, the answer came. No I wasn't ready to let go. I decided to go on living. And with that my illness turned and I was on the road to recovery.

ILLNESS IS A TIME OUT FOR THE BODY AND THE MIND

# Learning to Swim Through Molasses

This book flows easily at times, then all of a sudden it hits molasses. You know, it's that feeling when you want to move forward, but you can't. It's like trying to swim in molasses. Stuck to the ground. Sticky energy that just won't move.

A friend of mine shared with me this tidbit of wisdom.

- When I feel like the energy won't move, when my projects are stuck and no matter what I do I can't seem to budge the flow, when it feels like there is nothing for me to do, I've discovered there is a way out, he says. There is always some little thing that needs doing.

For him it could be changing the oil in the car, fixing a leaky faucet or doing the laundry.

I tried his approach. It works. Focus on the mundane everyday things in life, like ironing, weeding, catching up on mail, you know all the pesky little things we tend to push off. In my writing process I've discovered that cleaning out a closet or kitchen cupboard can unlock the creative juices. There is a wholeness to our process, to the living, that can't be ignored. I think we've missed that in our western approach to profits and productivity. We've lost sight of what moves us forward. Yes we can optimize and improve, but the know how of transforming to the next level has essentially been lost.

Seldom do we find innovation within the walls of established institutions. It is as if the very structure inhibits the free flow of energy and critical thinking. Innovation is less and less possible in downsized corporations, where the focus is short term, where all but the core production is outsourced. There is simply no room for dreamers and visionaries anymore in the old structures. But we haven't disappeared, we achieved escape velocity and do our thinking freelance.

SELDOM DO WE FIND INNOVATION WITHIN THE WALLS OF ESTABLISHED INSTITUTIONS

# In God We Trust

Common to all cultures is a belief in something greater than ourselves. Something that connects us with invisible threads. Something that has far greater wisdom than we as individuals possess. Something to worship and pray to with ceremonies for good health, harvest and luck.

We call this something by many names. Some call it God, some call it Allah, for some it's a name of a deity or guru. For many it doesn't have a name at all. We just know there is something bigger than us. Something unseen and benevolent to guide us through life here on earth.

It's that something we connect with in Z 2 A. When the healer says soften, let go, she is asking you to trust that something, that in the falling into the unknown you will be healed. That's God at work.

When the artist creates without thinking, just letting himself be guided by that unseen force, he is one with God. He is in that state we call I am. He is at one with Z 2 A.

As inspiration strikes and we find ourselves doing or saying things we didn't plan, we are one with Z 2 A. We've let in the voice of God. We've surrendered to the bigger than I force. Carl Jung talked about number 1 and number 2 personalites, where one was the ego and the other the higher self, or God force coming through. When we let the inspiration voice speak, we are truly wise.

The American motto is In God We Trust. Was it intended to be a Z 2 A country?

# More Books

**Meandering Mind** (2nd ed The Pathfinder Process) Eva has a lot of ideas. This time on relationships and organizations. Personal anecdotes liven up the story in between strategic planning and unconventional ideas for dating in the 21st century. Meandering Mind is an easy read, for such weighty subjects. Here you'll find lots of food for thought on a myriad of topics. This is the kind of book that is perfect for discussion groups. The material is presented with ease and an openness that leaves plenty of room for having your own thoughts, emotions and beliefs about each topic. If you interact with people from different parts of the globe, you'll appreciate Eva's views on the difference in mentality and culture of the US and Sweden.

**Secrets of Transformation** (2nd ed The Naked Truth) Misery Memoir Meets Self Help. So many people felt compelled to tell their stories of woe that a whole new genre was created: misery memoirs. But simply telling your story won't heal it or make it go away. Haven't we all listened to a friend go on and on about a past event, telling their story over and over, but it never seems to change. The emotions and hurt are still there. Every time! But, if you tell your story in such a way that you release and complete the emotional trauma, you heal and transform the event. It no longer carries a charge. It's done. By using her own dramatic life as an example, Eva illustrates how to do this, then shares the secrets behind the transformation. Since the release of The Naked Truth (the 1st edition of Secrets of Transformation) in 2003, readers say the book helped them heal or gain a new perspective on family dynamics, abuse, codependency, therapy, life... most found it a spell-binding read, unable to put it down until the very last page. This 2nd edition is much expanded (by a third). The story picks up five years later (life is never static, or done, is it?) with some surprising twists and turns. The section on how to tell your own healing story has a number of new chapters as well.

**God put a Dream in my Heart** There was something missing in the self help section of bookstores. A handbook for all of us trying to sort out our inner selves. When Eva was navigating through therapy sessions and personal growth workshops, she wished she'd had this book. What happens when you start to unlock your painful memories? How do you deal with them? How does the life energy connect with our emotions? What can you do between sessions and workshops to more efficiently deal with all that is stirred? A book full of insights, exercises and meditations. Lightened up with personal anecdotes.

*in Swedish* **Våga Leva** (The Courage to Live) Många läsare som hittat boken har hört av sig med entusiasm. De uppskattar att den är så personlig, så mänsklig och naturlig. De har känt sig inspirerade att äntligen ta det där steget ut i det okända... att våga satsa på den där drömmen som legat och viskat i deras hjärtan. Boken har väckt funderingar och tankar, bekräftat vad de innerst inne redan visste, eller skakat om i sättet att se på livet. Läsarna upplever att det är som jag sitter i soffan bredvid dem och vi samtalar över muggar med te, medan snöflingorna sakta dalar utanför i vintermörkret... Övningar och meditationer är samlade i slutet av boken, hela fyra timma i ljudboksversionen.

*in Swedish* **Livs Levande Eva** (Eva Live and in the Moment) När det var dags att göra ljudböcker, blev den första på svenska. Inspelad i nuet, i flödet, som om du vore med på ett enda långt Eva Party, får du följa med i funderingar, meditationer och berättelser ur Evas liv.

Print, audio and e-book editions available from Amazon and other internet retailers worldwide. More info and art on Eva's website

**www.evadillner.com**